JINGDEZHEN IMPERIAL KILN MUSEUM

Zhu Pei

JINGDEZHEN
IMPERIAL KILN MUSEUM

Zhu Pei

images
Publishing

Published in Australia in 2022 by
The Images Publishing Group Pty Ltd
ABN 89 059 734 431

Offices

Melbourne
Waterman Business Centre
Suite 64, Level 2 UL40
1341 Dandenong Road
Chadstone, Victoria 3148
Australia
Tel: +61 3 8564 8122

New York
6 West 18th Street 4B
New York City, NY 10011
United States
Tel: +1 212 645 1111

Shanghai
6F, Building C, 838 Guangji Road
Hongkou District, Shanghai 200434
China
Tel: +86 021 31260822

books@imagespublishing.com
www.imagespublishing.com

A catalogue record for this
book is available from the
National Library of Australia

Title: Jingdezhen Imperial Kiln Museum
Author: Zhu Pei
ISBN: 9781864709575

Printed by Shanghai Artron Art Printing Co., Ltd/Shanghai, China

IMAGES has included on its website a page for special notices in relation to this and its other publications.
Please visit www.imagespublishing.com

Every effort has been made to trace the original source of copyright material contained in this book. The publishers
would be pleased to hear from copyright holders to rectify any errors or omissions.

The information and illustrations in this publication have been prepared and supplied by Zhu Pei (Studio Zhu Pei)
and the contributors. While all reasonable efforts have been made to ensure accuracy, the publishers do not, under
any circumstances, accept responsibility for errors, omissions, and representations, express or implied.

Contents

Zhu Pei's Architecture

Steven Holl

I first met Zhu Pei in autumn 2003 at a café dinner organized by Li Hu at the then new 798 Art Zone in Beijing, China. The gigantic 1954 factory complex had been built by Bauhaus-influenced Germans (instead of in the Soviet style). In 1995, the Central Academy of Fine Arts (CAFA) in Beijing set up space in the defunct factory and by 2003, an artistic community of over thirty artists and publishers had collected there. I had asked Li Hu to introduce me to the most promising young architect, and he chose Zhu Pei. I remember the meeting well because the hard corn cob section I had tried to eat in the artist's café had broken off my tooth; I thought: I must be getting old.

In my book *Questions of Perception: A Phenomenology of Architecture*, 1993, Juhani Pallasmaa, Alberto Pérez-Gómez and I outline a general theory of architecture, which aims to emphasize the experiential dimensions of architecture. We argue for the importance of the "haptic realm" of material and detail in architecture, especially in a time of the predominating sheet rock and aluminum "junk space." Many of the points manifested in our text are brilliantly demonstrated in Zhu Pei's Imperial Kiln Museum in the central China city, Jingdezhen, in Jiangxi Province.

In our current digital era of object fixation, where many young architects aim only to make "iconic" architecture, the Imperial Kiln Museum is distinctly urban, with a deep connection to the city and site, and therefore, a specific cultural life and memory. In our time of climate change awareness, this work stands as an inspired architectural example with its north–south open vaults engaging cooling horizontal breezes, its attention to shade and shadow, and its poetic natural light. The porosity of its geometry engages people in the spatial energy of its overlapping perspectives.

My recent visit with Zhu Pei in Beijing, China, 2019. (Left to right: Anish Kapoor, Zhu Pei, myself, and Roberto Bannura)

Zhu Pei and I talking during a symposium in Beijing, China, 2019

The meticulous attention to detail and material in the work of Zhu Pei is celebrated here in a counterpoint of recycled kiln brick and new brick. When reflected in the museum's articulated landscape of mirror-like pools, this crucial dimension of architecture radiates, like music in a perfect acoustics hall, to amplify for future citizens and future students of architecture, a little utopian fragment in the center of the city of Jingdezhen; a masterpiece of architecture.

Rhinebeck, New York, United States

November 9, 2021

(Written on the 89th birthday of José Oubrerie, the last living protégé of Le Corbusier)

Steven Holl

Born in 1947 in Bremerton, Washington, United States, Steven Holl graduated from the University of Washington and pursued architecture studies in Rome in 1970. In 1976, he joined the Architectural Association in London and in 1977, established Steven Holl Architects. He was named by Time Magazine *as "America's Best Architect" for creating "buildings that satisfy the spirit, as well as the eye." He has realized cultural, civic, academic, and residential projects in the United States, as well as internationally. Steven has been recognized with architecture's most prestigious awards, notably the Praemium Imperiale Award for Architecture, the AIA Gold Medal, and the RIBA Jencks Award.*

Zhu Pei's Jingdezhen Imperial Kiln Museum in Jiangxi, China 2016–2020

Kenneth Frampton

As the architect's sketches indicate, this museum was envisaged from the outset not only as an archaeological metaphor, but also as an interstitial complex capable of mediating the severity of the local climate. The architect writes:

"… the long axis of the eight brick vaults is arranged in the north–south direction and the two ends of each vault are open. The arrangement of open and enclosed vaults not only blocks western sunlight … but also transforms each vault into a wind tunnel, allowing cool breezes to flow in, also capturing the frequent north–south winds during summer. At the same time, five sunken courtyards of different sizes and scales create the chimney effect, which functions vertically …"

The double-curved vaults appear from above as a topographic matrix integrated into the heart of an ancient industrial city that was once the center of porcelain production throughout the Ming dynasty. Situated as much below grade as above, the fragmented form of the museum is broken up not only by the gaps between the vaults, but also by a deliberate misalignment of their axes, engendering a rhythmically complex pattern of light and shade interspersed with five sunken courtyards open to the sky. The varying light of the vaults—brightly lit at their ends—is occasionally enlivened by long, narrow, horizontal openings allowed into the sides of the vaults. The light of the interior is further accented here and there by occasional cylindrical skylights let into the vaults, which refer to the observational apertures let into the sides of a traditional kiln. Constantly changing shafts of light—a result of the movement of the sun—unexpectedly serve to enliven the closed ends of certain vaults. Of this luminous iteration, the architect writes:

"The subtle changes in natural light, on the one hand, bring harmony to the museum with its

surrounding natural environment; on the other hand, it is also a medium that weaves people, exhibits, and architecture together."

Natural light is additionally augmented by adjustable spotlights that not only serve to illuminate specific exhibits, but also provide a dynamic mixture of cold and warm lighting throughout. These same lights are also capable of flood-lighting the inner surfaces of the vaults at night, giving their volumetric space a particularly dramatic character.

The building is inextricably enmeshed with the history of the site, having been finished inside and out with a virtually unending supply of used bricks that were accrued over time from the continual cyclical demolition and reconstruction of kilns, done so in order to maintain the high temperatures required for the firing of porcelain. These narrow, slightly polychromatic, unevenly burnt bricks are judiciously mixed with new bricks of the same character and proportion. These bricks, when laid carefully together, serve as the permanent formwork of the reinforced-concrete shell vaults, both within and without. As this revetment rises and falls over the curving form of the vaults, it assumes the character of a piece of textile that happens to be finished at its ends with two courses of stack-bonded bricks of a more flat, horizontal proportion. The same bricks, applied to the return edges of the vaults, evoke the image of a Roman arch. One notes that this tectonic trope is as removed from Chinese tradition as the barrel-vaulted vernacular of the Mediterranean is—from which the overall concept seems to have been derived. One has in mind, in this regard, Le Corbusier's barrel-vaulted housing, Roq et Rob, projected for Cap Martin in Roquebrune, France, in 1948. At the same time the expressive thrust of the vaults also evokes the sepulchral character of the Ming tombs situated on the outskirts of Beijing, China, the arcuated form often being associated with memorial constructions in Chinese culture.

To varying degrees, this work may be seen as being both <u>atectonic</u> and <u>tectonic</u>; atectonic in the sense that the bricks are only the formwork of the concrete shell vault, and <u>tectonic</u> in as much as the long narrow slots let into the sides of the vaults involve the use of either wide-span steel channels or equally long concrete-edge beams, these long lintels being cast integrally with the vault.

This work may also be seen as dialogical in other respects, not only in the contrast between the broad, stone-paved esplanade of the initial approach as opposed to the equally wide water gardens situated to either side, but also in the shift playing between the <u>mirage</u> of the museum as it is reflected in the water and the actual labyrinthine character of the complex at its lower level. There is also a conscious play between the metaphorically "ruined" character of the whole and the actual ruins of an original brick kiln, as this has been excavated in one of the sunken courtyards.

Judging from the amount of public space made available at the point of entry, this museum is as much a representational communal space as it is a museum in a didactic sense. This is evident, not only from the 130-seat auditorium that may be accessed independently from the entry esplanade, but also from the amount of space devoted to the foyer with views over the lower level at each end of the largest vault. The next vault in the spatial sequence, designated for a bookstore/café and tearoom overlooks the tranquil expanse of one of the water gardens. Each of these public spaces is enclosed by vaults that rise up and simultaneously encompass the upper and lower levels, with the latter in each instance serving as the primary exhibition space.

One notes, with respect to the main entrance, that the water gardens comprise shallow stretches of water lined with river pebbles, together with artfully placed rocks appearing just above the water line. In the smaller water garden, there is also a diminutive bamboo grove, the two together evoking the ethos of the traditional Chinese landscape. The next vault after the entrance foyer overlooks the excavated kiln and an atypical short vault sheltering an amphitheater, which is presumably used for orientation. The itinerary continues through a third, relatively narrow, vault housing the main stair leading down to the lower level, where the collection is mostly exhibited in free-standing glass cases that extend to the floor. Paradoxically, this arrangement seems to be at its best when the glass case is about the size of a small room, where the exhibit appears in the context of a more intimate scale.

Otherwise, there is a tendency of the more delicate pieces of porcelain to become lost against the monumentality of the vaults and this seems to be particularly the case when they are insufficiently emphasized by the spot lighting. One is reminded at this juncture of the work of Carlo Scarpa, where each museological element is treated as a micro tectonic piece in itself, the proportion and form of which mediates between the size of the object and the scale of the overall space. At the same time, this is a highly original and heroic work that restores the city of Jingdezhen to its honorific place in the history of Chinese culture.

Kenneth Frampton

Born in 1930, Kenneth Frampton was trained as an architect in the Architectural Association, United Kingdom (UK). He worked in the UK architecture office of Douglas Stephen & Partners from 1959 to 1965, and from 1962 to 1965, he was technical editor of the magazine Architectural Design. *Since then, he has been active as a critic and an academic. He is the author of many books and articles, including* Modern Architecture: A Critical History *(1980–2021),* Studies in Tectonic Culture *(1992),* Le Corbusier *(2001/2022),* Labor, Work, and Architecture *(2005),* A Genealogy of Modern Architecture *(2015), and* The Other Modern Movement *(2021). He is the Emeritus Ware Professor of Architecture at the Graduate School of Architecture, Planning and Preservation (GSAPP), Columbia University, New York, where he taught from 1972 to 2020. He has also taught at a number of architecture schools, including Eidgenössische Technische Hochschule (ETH), Zürich, École Polytechnique Fédérale de Lausanne (EPFL), Accademia di Architettura, Mendrisio, and the Royal College of Art, London, UK. He has been the recipient of numerous honorary degrees worldwide, and in 2021, he was awarded a Commander of the Order of the British Empire (CBE) honor in the UK for his service to architecture.*

The Archaeology of a Museum

Mohsen Mostafavi

Designing a contemporary building in the city of Jingdezhen in Jiangxi Province, China, can be fraught with challenges, particularly when that building is linked to the city's important historic, cultural, and artistic tradition of making porcelain.

Despite its relatively small population, Jingdezhen has long been China's capital of porcelain. The city's connection with ceramics dates back some two thousand years to the days of the Han dynasty (202 BCE–220 CE). Geographically, it was remote enough to remain untouched by the conflicts that would stall the development of porcelain-making in other regions; at the same time, it also had an abundance of the necessary resources for manufacture, such as fine china stone, or petuntse, forests for the supply of wood to fire the many kilns, and nearby rivers for water. During the Ming dynasty (1368–1644), Jingdezhen's status as China's largest producer of ceramic artifacts was enhanced when it was assigned the responsibility of making "imperial porcelain" for the emperor and his household. The first Imperial Kiln was constructed in Jingdezhen as early as 1369.

While the city is still best known for its manufacture of porcelain and ceramics, many of its old workshops and kilns have been demolished or have turned into ruins. But there are some, mainly in the city's central district, that have been restored as part of the tangible heritage of the region. These structures simultaneously showcase the old traditions of the city and act as attractions for the growing tourism industry.

In recent years, Jingdezhen has broadened its manufacturing base beyond porcelain to include, among others, the automotive and aviation industries. For example, the city has become a major producer of helicopters. The push toward modernization, combined with an ambitious local political leadership aware of the value of the city's history makes Jingdezhen one of the more unusual smaller cities in China. How, then, to acknowledge the importance of conserving historic artifacts linked to the manufacture of porcelain, while also promoting a contemporary and forward-looking agenda? Inevitably, this is one of the challenges confronted by the design of the new Imperial Kiln Museum.

In China, the authenticity of a "historic building" can be inferred from the replication of that building or the restoration of that building to its original state—embodied by the term *yuanzhenxing*—or through the recognition of its various states of transformation over time—referred to as *zhenshixing*. These concepts can also offer a perspective on contemporary architecture and its relation to historic precedents. For example, how might a new building negotiate its relationship with the past, while also acknowledging its contemporaneity?

In this schema, the link with the past, or its replication, can be either literal or analogical. One relies on the mimicking or duplicating of shapes and forms, whereas the other is more interpretative in character. In the latter case, while the homage or reference to the past might still be recognizable, the form of the design as realized would need to transcend the original time of its referent, by belonging to the present. It is a building's programmatic, spatial, and material characteristics that contribute to its temporal resonance. So, how might the position of the new museum be characterized with regard to these issues?

The Imperial Kiln Museum occupies an unusually significant site that is rich with historic remnants of porcelain manufacturing. It is not purely the location for a building dedicated to the history of porcelain and ceramics, but is as much an archaeological site.

The project consists of a series of vaulted brick structures, reminiscent of traditional Chinese kilns. Though different in size, these structures are rhythmically arranged adjacent to each other, like notes on a sheet of music. Similarly, their formal variations and spacings, as a cluster, produce a visually coherent field. In this way, they achieve integration and an overall unity despite their scalar difference. Still, the placement of the vaulted structures remains as contingent on the archaeological conditions of the site as it does on the distribution and sequence of the program within the building.

While from the outside the museum appears as a series of single-story structures, it occupies three floors, two of them located below ground. After entering the first permanent exhibition space on the ground floor, the visitor descends to the lower level to view the rest of the artifacts on display in the other permanent exhibition spaces. The location and datum of the lower-level galleries are akin to that of an archaeological site where the artifacts on display might have been found. Yet, the artifacts are on view within the pristine walls of a gallery. The space can be imagined, both literally and metaphorically, as a site both excavating and unraveling the archaeological terrain, and covering it up; entombing it for the purpose of display. Such is the conflictual nature of building on the site of historical remains.

The complexities of this condition are explicitly highlighted in one of the central structures of the building, which appears to have been "pulled apart" to reveal the ruins of an early porcelain workshop. The visitor first encounters these physical remains of the past on entering the exhibition space from the lobby of the museum. Caught between the permanent exhibition space on one side, and an amphitheater on the other, the character of the ruins—as an artifice—is heightened by one's awareness of the potential gaze of the onlooker from the amphitheater opposite. The juxtaposition with the amphitheater denaturalizes the image of the ruins. It is not just the onlookers who view the ruins, with the museum beyond, but the amphitheater as well; a set of relations that juxtaposes the present with the past and the past with the present.

The museum contains other instances when the internal and timeless continuities of the experience of the museum—which are in some ways not so dissimilar to the timeless mandates and experiences in a casino—are consciously interrupted by the longitudinal direction of views from the vaulted structures of the building. This relationship between inside and outside is choreographed through a series of external sunken gardens that also help to mediate the relationship between the museum and the surrounding historic neighborhood. Two large pools of water placed on either side of the museum entrance complement the visual and sensorial qualities of the building. These external elements are as much concerned with the real and apparent porosity of the museum, for both visitors and passersby, as they are with the museum's desire to create a carefully conceived open environment in dialogue with natural systems.

These connections between inside and outside, made possible by the museum's scale, as well as its formal and material qualities, extend to the larger urban context. The height of the museum's vaulted structures is limited to a maximum of 39.4 feet (12 meters), in compliance with local planning regulations for the historic neighborhood. In addition to its respect for the surrounding historic urban fabric, the museum also acknowledges the large vertical presence of the six-story

Longzhu or Dragon's Pearl Pavilion opposite its main entrance. The original pavilion, built during the Tang dynasty (618–907), played an important role in the production of ceramics for the Imperial family, but had fallen into ruin. What stands there now is a full-scale restoration from 1987, carried out in a manner consistent with the concept of *yuanzhenxing*, which is the reconstruction of the presumed original.

It is, therefore, an irony that a major contemporary cultural building, innovative in its design response to current programmatic requirements should be subjected to height restrictions in deference to a pavilion that was almost wholly rebuilt not so long ago. In this context, which of the two buildings is more authentic? The reconstructed Longzhu Pavilion or the new Imperial Kiln Museum?

The question of authenticity, especially with regard to the public's reception of this authenticity, is full of complexity. While the pavilion is fundamentally a reconstruction, it still symbolizes the long history of the city and its associations with the highly sophisticated artistic and craft-based traditions of porcelain manufacture. The pavilion also embodies a reverence for the architectural ideas and construction methods used in its original state, albeit now replicated within the changed circumstances of contemporary construction. Still, if we were to follow cultural theorist Jean Baudrillard's argument about the concept of simulacrum, the Longzhu Pavilion would be viewed less as a question of duplication, and more as a question of "substituting the sign of the real for the real." However, in the context of everyday life, supposed historic artifacts are rarely considered in such forensic detail. The narrative of the pavilion's symbolism overshadows the question of its authenticity.

The Imperial Kiln Museum also engages with the idea of replication, and in a manner that is at times seemingly even "less authentic" than the rebuilding of the pavilion. To create its homage to the brick vaults of Jingdezhen's historic kilns, the museum does not use the original structural brickwork, but instead relies on a concrete vault for its structural stability between two layers of brickwork: one above, and one below the concrete shell. This approach, enforced by seismic code requirements, raises questions about the true status of the museum's "brick structures," as it does of the hidden sandwiched concrete formwork that imitates the shape of the city's original brick vaults.

Do such deviations from the original make the architecture of the museum inauthentic? Or are they manifestations of the challenges architecture faces when it confronts contemporary realities such as program and code requirements, while also engaging with the anamnesis of earlier precedents?

Perhaps, the Imperial Kiln Museum is closer in spirit to the concept of *zhenshixing* and its recognition of the discontinuous and disjunctive dimension of an architectural artifact's transformations in time. This is the true value of the speculative and experimental contribution of the Imperial Kiln Museum. The project also provides a worthy and productive path for how contemporary Chinese architecture might confront its own histories, as well as futures.

Mohsen Mostafavi

Mohsen Mostafavi is the Alexander and Victoria Wiley Professor of Design at Harvard Graduate School of Design and a Harvard University Distinguished Service Professor. He is author and co-author of numerous publications, including On Weathering: The Life of Buildings in Time; Surface Architecture; Approximations: The Architecture of Peter Märkli; Structure as Space: Engineering and Architecture in the Works of Jürg Conzett and His Partners; Ecological Urbanism; Ethics of the Urban: The City and the Spaces of the Political; *and* Portman's America and Other Speculations. *He is currently conducting a multiyear research project on architecture and urbanization in Japan (see japanstory.org).*

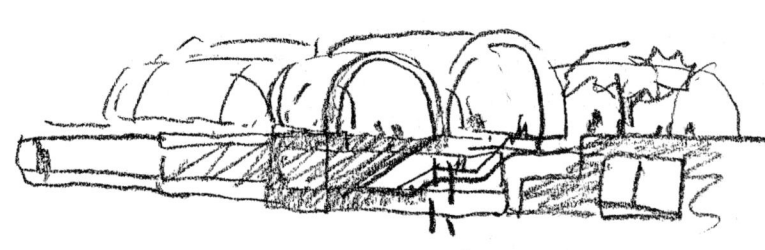

Artistic Conception of *Luan Yao*: Between Uncertainty and Doubting

Zhou Rong

Contemporary Doubting in a Hypercomplex World

The site of Jingdezhen Imperial Kiln Museum is located in an extremely complex environment that seems constituted as a metaphor of the ages: old alleys versus the sudden rise of commercial buildings; ancient ruins of kilns versus reconstructions of traditional dwellings; fine-painted cornices versus modern minimalist exhibition architecture. These fragmented pieces of time and space emerged and aggregated to form a radial fault of urban geography, however, a clear structure of cultural narrative has yet to be completed.

The highly complicated location of the Imperial Kiln Museum reflects the hypercomplex world that architect faces—the vision of orderliness promised by modern utopia has already become dilapidated, and capitalism, technicism, society, and information have agitated power turbulences. The accumulated experiential equipment and historical imaginations indulged in by human civilization over the past 5,000 years are collapsing, and for the first time, the future is transforming into a highly uncertain "black hole" of cognition, devouring every "certain" solution.

Architects possess neither consciousness and insight, nor vigilance and preparation when it comes to the inherent "certainty crisis" of the contemporary world. Today, most architectural practices still linger in an ideological phase of assertion, as if they are absolutely certain about the truth of the universe, and they might preach to the "chaotic" world in a top-down approach for the purpose of a better future. The world has changed without notice, but the principle of the world has long veered from the orbit of modernist ideology and its value range. Modernity can no longer act as the anchor point that carries permanence for contemporary people; also, the new framework of "meaning" is still searching for its foundation. Against this backdrop, any spatial structures made by architects to fortify the old orders all seem fallacious and frivolous.

From my perspective, the most remarkable intellectual contribution of the Jingdezhen Imperial Kiln Museum is the "doubting" attitude that it conveys toward the orderly modern world, which was revealed by Zhu Pei at the stage of the conceptual design. As a leading architect who has intensively participated in establishing spatial paradigms in China over the past two decades, Zhu Pei has become a beneficiary with remarkable achievements; an insider who is entrusted with the significant task of maintaining the system. However, after years of introspection and contemplation, he began to strongly doubt the principles of modern architecture in which he had long believed, and practiced. This doubting has manifested as a kind of Hamlet irresolution in the design of the Imperial Kiln Museum.

As the museum faces an extremely complicated environment around the site, Zhu Pei knew that the new architecture would need to have a cognitive structure of complexity and a luxuriant visual attraction in order to have the power to unite the surroundings. At the same time, he also needed to avoid inserting an over-designed modern structure into the fabric of the existing neighborhood, where the newcomer might cause strong contrast and conflict with the many accidental fragments that have accumulated through time. Only by doing so would he be able to achieve harmony out of the chaos and embrace the power of the complex surroundings and turn them into a life spring to support their own vitality.

Water is one of the most fluid properties in the world. In order to reach a state of harmony between the new architecture and the complex surrounding boundary, Zhu Pei has creatively adopted a "spatial liquefied" strategy: he sees the site as the water surface, and divides the entire architecture into more than a dozen independent long, narrow vaults—varied in sizes—which look like a cluster of boats with black awning gathered on the shore. When the wind blows and the water ripples, these "floating" vaults respond to each other through a very natural interval and arrangement. They are parallel to each other, but also misaligned, like how real boats are as they sway on the water. They appear to be arranged in a certain order, but also escape from a precisely arranged geometric framework. Though they seem like they are arranged in a random layout, an extremely subtle and delicate ingenuity in design can be found in every detail. This liquefied space structure, which softens the rational stiffness, is loose and flowing. It has neither a certain centrality, nor clear boundary. The interface between interior and exterior is blur, which provides various possibilities for visitors when it comes to exploring and wandering. According to the conventional principles of modern architecture, the museum is undoubtedly inefficient or even *anti*-efficient, but it unexpectedly brings a sense of richness that most modern architecture cannot provide, as well as some inexpressible contemporaneity.

If the most prevalent feature of the world today is overwhelming uncertainty, then, unfortunately, the architectural industry is scarcely ready for the uncertain and rapidly changing world. Denial, rejection, and evasion seem to be the trilogy of stress response for most architects when facing this new world of uncertainty.

As a sharp contrast, what Zhu Pei shows in the design of the Imperial Kiln Museum is his suspicion and rebellion against the "Deterministic Utopia" that has been promised and falsely relied upon by modernist architecture. From Zhu Pei's perspective, uncertainty means taking disturbing risks, but it also leads to a thrilling freedom. There is a field of "doubting" and uncertainty that exists between the polarities of "certainty." It is a field of creativity—lonely and vast—that bestows immeasurable possibilities of forms and meanings that have not yet been explored. Given this, then perhaps employing uncertainty as a resource of creativity, and doubting as an origin of design should be the features to distinguish contemporary architecture from classical modernist architecture.

Jingdezhen Imperial Kiln Museum is an architecture of doubting and wandering. On the one hand, the architect established a clear rational structure, but on the other, he gently "messed" it and "wiped" it. When wandering through the spaces of the museum, one will experience a brief confusion, as well as a slight melancholy from time to time, moving between order and disturbance. These omnipresent cognitive voids lend blank patches and tiny wrinkles to the seemingly smooth thought and make the circuitous and rhythmical spatial narrative richer and more profound by breaking through a conventional language interpretation. Although the design maintains harmony in its formality and tones, the overall complex still presents a rare sense of flickering in cognition: Interwoven with denying; existing instead of solving. There is neither definite methodology, nor ultimate conclusion; it is just like a contemporary world that is acquired at will.

"Chineseness" with Inherent Body Tenderness

For thousands of years, the kilns, with their never-ending flames and smoke wisping forth day and night, have been the soul of the city of Jingdezhen (in Jiangxi Province, China), the porcelain capital. The construction of a traditional kiln, known as *luan yao*, was a unique local craft that was purposed to build and mend a kiln. When building the kiln and chimney, the craftspeople neither used scaffolding, nor used the ruler and hanging line. They relied solely on their hands, eyes, and accumulated experience to mold and erect the irregular yet delicate vaults of the kiln.

If you look closely at the inside of a traditional kiln that has been built by the skilled hands of kiln craftspeople, you will see that it is undoubtedly magnificent, unconsciously attracting your eyes and thoughts with its construction marvels. Unlike modern spaces designed by architects through principles of rationality, the character of the creations of *luan yao* craftsmanship is anchored in the iterative trial-and-error traces, which result from the consistent entanglement between the skin and the natural substance, and the push-and-pull forces of the wrist and gravity. Uneven stacks of non-standardized bricks that are connected and rectified by countless micro contingencies form a bodily space manifested as a coherent whole. Although no specific part is perfect on its own, the space is teeming with a "body temperature order" bestowed by the human palm.

Zhu Pei has always been deeply fascinated with traditional kiln construction (*luan yao*) as an exclusive craftsmanship that grapples with experience and uncertainty, which enlightens him, and it has led him to rekindle the connection between the human body and the substance of the museum. To achieve such a goal, architects should unlearn the rational doctrines that have long occupied their training and rediscover the art of craft through raw sensations, rather than the disciplined eye. Re-*cognizing* the conventional design paradigm, Zhu Pei creatively applies continuous non-uniform section vaults as the prototype to form space in the design of the Imperial Kiln Museum.

Throughout the history of modern architecture, there have been numerous cases that utilize aggregated vaulted modules to obtain extraordinary interior spaces. The Kimbell Art Museum, designed by Louis I. Kahn in the early 1970s, and Sangath Office, completed by Balkrishna Vithaldas Doshi in 1981, are exemplars of those endeavors. Yet, an examination of the underlying design logic behind the two works reveals that both the cycloid vaults in Kimbell Art Museum and the barrel vault in Sangath Office create an entity of spaces that are driven by the simplification and rationalization of geometrical principles, establishing "a deified rational order" that transcends day-to-day experience.

However, the spiritual connotation of the "continuous non-uniform section vaults" in the Imperial Kiln Museum, inspired by the traditional kiln construction process, is quite different from that in a deified rational order. In fact, the seemingly unified vaults of the museum are unscientific structures that exhibit countless minute formal variations, and do not conform to any standardized or calculated template. Like in the *luan yao* construction process, the architect was immersed in making forms through employing the "palm" of his thinking and emotion. He "felt" and molded the special shape of each vault in his mind and in the physical model. The consequential trajectories of spaces cannot be uniformly defined by mathematical formulas; weaved into light and shadow, the substance unveils itself here and there, in its most preferable temporal and spatial conditions, as naturally as possible.

To reflect and enhance the sense of humanness that exists in traditional kiln craftsmanship, Zhu Pei used recycled kiln bricks with "kiln sweat"[1] glazed textures from abandoned local kilns and randomly mixed them with new kiln bricks on the inner and outer façades of his design, amplifying

1. A type of crystalline compound made up of wood ash and vaporized clay minerals that accumulates on kiln bricks from years of ceramic firing.

the uncertainty created by the "continuous non-uniform section vaults." Hence, architecture is no longer an unnegotiable and dominant force, but an empathetic friend with a sensitive soul that can be felt, relied on, and communicated with.

These scattered vaults, which seem to emerge freely from the soil, display the vital signs of breath and temperature. Like a pride of creatures/lifeforms resting at ease, they appear gentle, serene, and open for everyone to access. From classical architecture enthusiasts to modern architecture fans, to Chinese civilians and Western architects, the building provides everyone with a cordial and touching sense of familiarity. Although the continuous non-uniform section vault is a recent invention of the architect, it does not present the sense of strangeness or the arrogant aggression demonstrated in some new contemporary formal constructions. There it simply stands, perched between the new and the old, the Chinese and the Western. It does not deliberately flaunt or flatter, but slowly extends its warmth into time and space, and people's lives.

For more than a century, architectural "Chineseness" has always been a polarized alternative in the binary structure between China and the West. To represent and express the specificity and autonomy of "Chineseness," Chinese architects oftentimes unconsciously transition into a nervous mindset, eager to draw a clear line set apart from the West, and to be distinguished from the modern. This exclusive Chineseness, existing apart from the system of contemporary civilization, prohibits Chinese architecture to be promoted globally as a cultural currency. For this reason, the inclusion of Neo-Chinese craftsmanship in the design of the Jingdezhen Imperial Kiln Museum is particularly appealing. After all, though ideas and cultures vary, emotions and bodily expressions are shared by all.

The Urban Community: The Magnetic Field for Spirit and the Anchoring Point for Meaning

The culture of a city is not an unpredictable deposit; it needs to "be seen, be confirmed, and be spread" through various visible methods. In that way, a city can be sublimated from a physical shell into a humanistic community with a spiritual core and emotional connections. For the contemporary humanistic community that needs continuous development, the significance of a city cannot stagnate in the relics of its glorious past. The spiritual energy contained in traditional creations must be revealed, stimulated, reshaped, and spread through new constructions of contemporaneity.

In the past, the kilns with their blazing fire that existed all over Jingdezhen symbolized prosperity and pride. During intervals in production, the space inside a spare porcelain kiln provided citizens with all kinds of amenities for living. These past scenes have long subsided to become the collective public memories of the city. Due to the rapidly declining porcelain industry, the city needs to transform as a whole from economic, social, and cultural perspectives. At this critical historic point of carrying forward the past and forging ahead into the future, the matter of how to recondense the spiritual core of the urban humanistic community through rebuilding identity is the trump card that can break the obsolescence and reshape the fate of Jingdezhen.

The completion of the Imperial Kiln Museum in Jingdezhen, to a large extent, has restored the city's vitality, boosted its increasingly fading culture, and led the reconstruction process of the city's cultural space. A wise architect understands that the power of an architecture is not limited to just the form of material space, but extends way beyond the physical imagination; it is a spiritual magnetic field with a broad, far radial impact. A great architect can perceive the resonance frequency of the humanistic community and discern the secret of reassuring urban folk. Essentially, in this modern world based on urban civilization, the city must be responsible for providing a holistic system for spiritual habitation. The meanings of our life are deeply anchored with the city; thus, architecture design has to reserve solid anchor points accordingly.

It is rare for an architecture to enter the canons of contemporary architecture the day it is revealed to the public. The Jingdezhen Imperial Kiln Museum is one of such few masterpieces. In this era that is full of uncertainty, doubting has become mainstay, redundancy has become the significance, contemplation has become attitude, and ambiguity has become goodwill. As long-standing carriers of civilization through time, all architecture may need to be recultivated, like this museum, in order to navigate and rise from the booming growth of complexity of the contemporary world.

Zhou Rong

A well-known scholar, critic, and curator in the fields of Chinese contemporary architecture, urbanization, and public art, Zhou Rong obtained his Master in Design Studies from Harvard University, and PhD from Tsinghua University. He is associate professor of the School of Architecture, Tsinghua University, and visiting professor of the Central Academy of Fine Arts (CAFA). He is deputy editor in chief of World Architecture, *an editorial board member of many international and domestic professional media, founder of the original knowledge media "Global Knowledge Lei Feng," and co-creator of the City for Humanity Awards.*

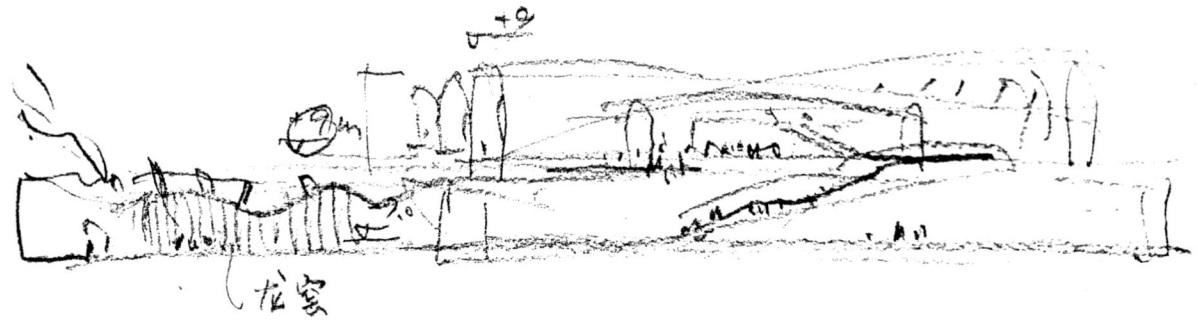

龙家

A Masterpiece of Cultural Architecture Spanning History and Reality

Li Xiangning

The achievements of contemporary Chinese architecture over the last three decades have been concomitant with the rapid expansion of Chinese cities. Due to that, reflecting the high density of urbanization has become an objective reality that architects face. In recent years, though, the creation of architectural works that combine with natural scenery or a humanistic context in a less dense and more vast natural environment outside the metropolis has been a conceptual leap of architects with more subjective projection. Another challenge that architects must face is the changing urban and rural environment, which, in the last three decades, has continuously disconnected us from our history and traditions. If contemporary architecture loses its cultural foundations, the situation will inevitably become a dire scene of making bricks without straw. Be it within cities that have suffered the trauma of large-scale demolition and reconstruction, or among professionals in contemporary Chinese architectural practice and academic studies, cultural architecture that can truly span history and contemporary reality possesses historic value.

Jingdezhen, a time-honored city of Jiangxi Province in southern China, has not only landscapes of mountains and rivers and urban scenes veiled by enshrouding mist to the south of the Yangtze River, but also ruins of kilns that depict the glory of the ancient Chinese porcelain culture from the Song and Yuan dynasties to the Ming and Qing dynasties. Today, the life of people in Jingdezhen is still related to ceramics processing: jiggering, glazing, painting, and firing. Most memories in the daily lives of ordinary people revolve around the abandoned kilns or the physical memory of embracing a hot kiln brick in the cold winter. The experience and techniques of the masonry craftspeople who built the old kilns by hand are also waiting for opportunities of a revival, even if they be modest ones. With the urban development of the last two decades, the porcelain capital that was born from the flames and ashes of kilns has been rejuvenated with the cultural glory of its past. However, the construction quality and cultural reflections of recently constructed buildings in the process of economic recovery could hardly add up to match the past status of the old porcelain capital city in the world cultural landscape. But, today, the city glitters in the brilliant glow of ceremony and celebration bestowed by the completion and opening of the Jingdezhen Imperial Kiln Museum. The museum, designed by Zhu Pei, highlights Jingdezhen in a moment of time in the development process of Chinese contemporary culture and contemporary architecture in the world.

Whether we are observing from the top of the pavilion-style building on the west side of the museum, or enjoying the model made of Jingdezhen's unique shadowy celadon outside the exhibition hall, we can see the whole presentment of the Imperial Kiln Museum. The space composition is featured with a metaphorical atmosphere: the main body is a series of long arched structures that seem to remind of the spatial prototype of brick kilns. Every single structure of this series is basically arranged to the same orientation, which maintains the simple unity of architectural language; both sides of the structures are open to the outdoor landscape. While the scattered geometric forms appear like dices that were thrown and landed randomly, they also present as a combination that is naturally formed on an archaeological site through historical deposition. The sunken buildings and the sporadic archaeological sites between the forms speak a more coherent language that reveals the metaphor. The shallow water pools around the main structures reflect the volume of the museum and also form a shallow moat, delimiting a clear boundary between the museum and the surroundings. The moat also comes through as symbolizing a guardian, reflecting the historical importance of the museum and the Imperial Kiln ruins it overlays and protects. There is no usual boundary wall, in the typical sense, around the museum; the waters and the sunken parts become the invisible boundaries, which consistently maintain the physical continuity of the space and visual continuity of the landscape.

New red-face bricks mixed together with old bricks with black and shiny "kiln sweat" form a dark red surface texture. The material, determined after careful selection and numerous site sample comparisons, completely covers the interior and exterior walls of the whole museum. This ensures the interpretation of traditional brick kiln structures and the red bricks commonly used in such kilns. It also establishes the coordination of the color of the vaults with the glazed tiles of the pavilion-style building on the opposite grass slope, as well as forms a certain color contrast with the ancient houses with white walls and gray tiles and the newly built high-rise residential buildings around the site. The museum, therefore, integrates into this complex field that spans time and space, and which overlaps the new and the old. In such an environment, the Imperial Kiln Museum acts more like a riveted hub of time and space, linking many elements, while highlighting the special historical value of the site.

Entering the building complex, the dominant design of utilizing north–south ventilation makes each structure a long, arched vault. Skylights that mimic smoke holes, together with the artificial lighting of the vaults jointly create an image of a sky that floats in between being real and illusory. The whole interior is shaped like caves, or more appropriately, the inner parts of brick kilns. It is in such spaces that the porcelain treasures of the Song and Yuan dynasties are preserved and displayed; the underground level provides stable and controllable indoor lighting for the exhibition. The interior is reminiscent of the clear and deep space created by Louis I. Kahn in the Phillips Exeter Academy Library using red bricks, concrete, wood, and glass. The deep and quiet spaces are interrupted by the skylights on the ceilings of the vaults from time to time, and the natural light from the connection indicates the direction of the display flow line. A small group of interior spaces that connect upward and downward provide a multilayered space that offers a panoramic view of the exhibits on the ground floor and underground floor, and also strengthens the sense of openness and depth of the exhibition halls on each layer. The rhythm of the interior spaces is well controlled by the architect: the climaxes and pauses established by every single exhibition hall through the series of vaults, mixed with several underground inner courtyards, create a connection between the underground exhibition spaces and the landscape of the outdoor courtyards (a frequent Chinese cultural image) where the fragments of the Imperial Kiln ruins excavated by archaeologists have been preserved. A visual connection between the indoor ancient porcelain exhibits and the historical space where they have been excavated from is established, and a deep dialogue between the new museum buildings and the Imperial Kiln ruins is further facilitated.

As a practicing "Architecture of Nature," the Imperial Kiln Museum features the organic integration of ecological performance with the surroundings. The relationship between the museum and nature lies not only in a visual sense and cultural imagery, but also in the flow and free exchange of indoor and outdoor air. From the perspective of environmental performance, the museum has been created as an architectural model integrating nature and a historical context. As an initiator of the philosophy and practical strategy of "Architecture of Nature," the museum undoubtedly demonstrates Zhu Pei's ingenuity in its spatial structuring: The whole museum is designed as a porous and spongiform building complex; the north–south vaulted spaces and outdoor courtyards transition from one to another; the repeated indoor and outdoor alternating layout makes the museum closer to nature; the linearly arranged long vaults act as open and ventilated tunnels; and the sunken inner courtyards planted with bamboo groves create an effect similar to chimney drafts. All these together provide a comfortable environment with cool winds without air conditioning, even in the hot summers of Jingdezhen. The combination of traditional architectural designs and nature can improve environmental performance and level-up comfort without technical facilities that impose high investments. The museum, itself, is an architectural practice of design intelligence and an outstanding example of contemporary architecture that successfully addresses ecological and energy-saving demands.

The all-round openness of the Imperial Kiln Museum will become an important node in the urban development history of Jingdezhen City. The museum is not only the container of the exhibition, but also the exhibition piece, like the porcelain treasures on display excavated from the archaeological site it sits on. It has become a visiting destination for cultural and design professionals, as well as appreciators of art and culture. Not only has it, quite quickly, graced the covers of important international and Chinese architectural magazines like *Arquitectura Viva*, *Architectural Record*, and *Architecture China*, it was also featured as the main work in the Museum of Modern Art (MoMA) exhibition "Reuse, Renew, Recycle: Recent Architecture from China," for which I served as the curator consultant. The Imperial Kiln Museum has written a historical chapter in the contemporary inheritance of Chinese architectural culture. The cultural form linking tradition and contemporary language created by Zhu Pei in this museum will be an important milestone not only for the city of Jingdezhen, but also in the history of global contemporary architecture.

Li Xiangning

Li Xiangning is dean and full professor of history, theory, and criticism at Tongji University's College of Architecture and Urban Planning. He is a member of CICA (Comité International des Critiques d'Architecture) and secretary general of the China Architectural Society Architectural Criticism Committee. He is also the editor in chief of the international magazine Architecture China *and was a visiting professor of Architecture at Harvard Graduate School of Design in 2016. He was curator of the Chinese Pavilion at the 2018 Venice Biennale and is the curatorial advisor of the ongoing exhibition at MoMA on contemporary Chinese architecture.*

wind flow

hot air

sun

E

summer

S

wind flow

W

Studies of solar and wind at Jean schein

wind tunnels → vaults, horizontal

Chimney effect → vertical courtyard

Creative Thinking

Site

The Imperial Kiln Museum is located adjacent to the Imperial Kiln ruins of the Ming and Qing dynasties, at the heart of the historic district of Jingdezhen, Jiangxi Province, China, on the east side of the Chang River. The museum is surrounded by buildings of different ages—from traditional residential dwellings and private kilns of the Ming and Qing dynasties, to factories built after 1949, to commercial residential towers of the late 1990s—and the rich and diversified urban fabric has created an extremely unique and profound historical and cultural context.

Today's Imperial Kiln Factory site is an open field. The buildings that were on the grounds no longer exist, which is particularly unusual in the high-density historical city center. The site now stands as a testimony of the past glories of the place, inviting endless imaginations about the past inspired by the ruins buried underground. The Imperial Kiln Museum is a theme museum; its main exhibition content is the extremely precious porcelain excavated from the Imperial Kiln site.

The original architectural conception was developed along two main points: root and contemporaneity. Root refers to the specific natural, geographical, and climatic conditions of a region, as well as the specific survival mode and culture that bred from it. Contemporaneity is an attempt to subvert the traditional concept of existing museums and create a new museum experience. On the one hand, it is a rethinking of the "Chinese character" and "international character;" on the other hand, it is also an experiment about the ideology of "Architecture of Nature."[1]

The site-specific design of the Imperial Kiln Museum incorporates the understanding of the site, and the complex analysis involves such scopes as urban study, archaeology, anthropology, climate, and other related fields.

1. Design philosophy of Zhu Pei. A contemporary architectural theory based on traditional Chinese natural philosophy and explores the relationship between the tradition and the contemporary.

Jingdezhen is known as a city that was "born because of kilns and flourished because of porcelain." People came from afar to settle down near the mountains and live close to rivers, dedicating their lives to building kilns and making porcelain. The trinity of porcelain kilns, workshops, and dwellings constituted the basic unit of the city. Based on this, the prototype and structure of the city were thus established. Narrow lanes ran east to west, linking thousands of private kilns, to lead straight to the Chang River. In the hot summer, the narrow lanes extending under the eaves of the dwellings provided spaces that were fully shaded and sheltered from the sun and rain. The old city's craftspeople would push their wheelbarrows along these lanes between the brick kilns and the Chang River to dispatch newly made porcelain and return with more clay and firewood. The main streets of the city have always been parallel with the Chang River, running from north to south, linking markets together to form a busy bazaar. Local residences are built to the Huizhou typology, with vertical courtyards, enclosed pitched roofs to gather water, and long eaves extending out of the façade. In summer, the eaves provide shade and create a chimney effect, which guarantees good natural ventilation. The urban layout and architectural style not only reflect the local lifestyle, but also display the local long-standing wisdom of the people in dealing with the hot and humid climate.

Site location (opposite page) and bird's-eye view

Traditional *lilongs* (above) and vertical courtyard (right)

Traditional *lilongs*

Brick kiln workshop

Brick kiln

Brick kiln workshop

Brick kiln workshop

Ideas

The structural form of the Imperial Kiln Museum building draws inspiration from the old traditional local brick kilns of Jingdezhen. Different from the Roman arch, a traditional brick kiln is not a simple geometric shape, but made of a set of complex double-curved surfaces, which conveys the typical characteristics of the oriental vault. When constructing a traditional brick kiln, kiln craftspeople did not use scaffolding; rather, the building was completed with the assistance of gravity, by taking advantage of the dislocation of the bricks. If you were to carefully observe and study the construction process of the double-curved vault *(luan yao)*, you will be surprised to find that olden-day craftspeople ingeniously broke down the extremely complex double-curved vault that resembles the shape of an eggshell into countless single-curved surfaces by making countless horizontal cuttings along the long axis, in which the thickness of the cuts is the exact thickness of the kiln brick itself. These craftspeople used their fingers to control the dislocation of every single-curved surface to complete the construction of the entire double-curved vault. This method, though seemingly ancient, is the same process we use today to generate double-curved forms using the computer.

Brick kilns not only form the origin of the city of Jingdezhen, but also the living and public spaces of local people. They preserve the warm memory that is inseparable from life in the city in the old days—during harsh winter days, a child would pick up a hot brick from a brick kiln on their way to school, place it in their schoolbag, and hold the bag in their arms to keep themselves warm throughout the day. In winter, schools were also often moved close to the warm porcelain kilns; in summer, when the brick kilns were "shut" and not used, they provided humid, cool air naturally, and became gathering places for children, young people, and the elderly to interact, play, and pass time. The broken walls of these kiln ruins that have passed down immortal memories from generation to generation are the natural source of creative inspiration for the Imperial Kiln Museum. The unique oriental vault as the prototype of the porcelain kiln, as well as the everlasting memory of the kiln bricks, has shaped the consanguinity of the kilns, porcelain, and the people. The brick kiln has long been an important part of the cultural memory and urban life in Jingdezhen, and it has naturally become the structural form of the Imperial Kiln Museum.

Restoration of a traditional kiln

Restoration of a traditional kiln

Restoration of a traditional kiln

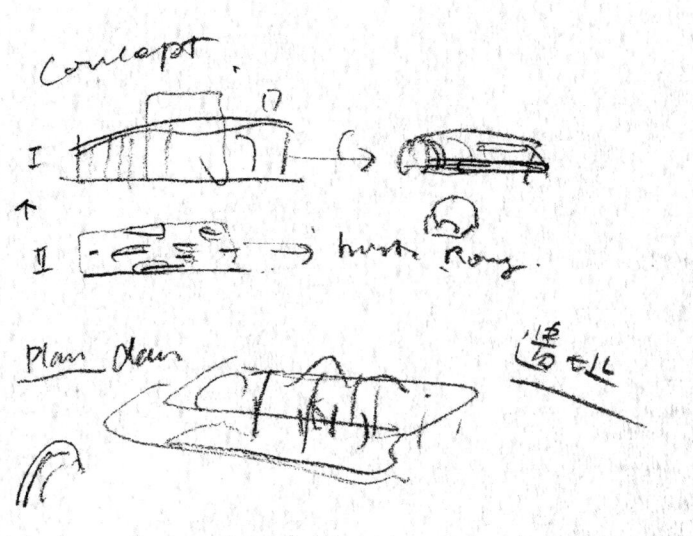

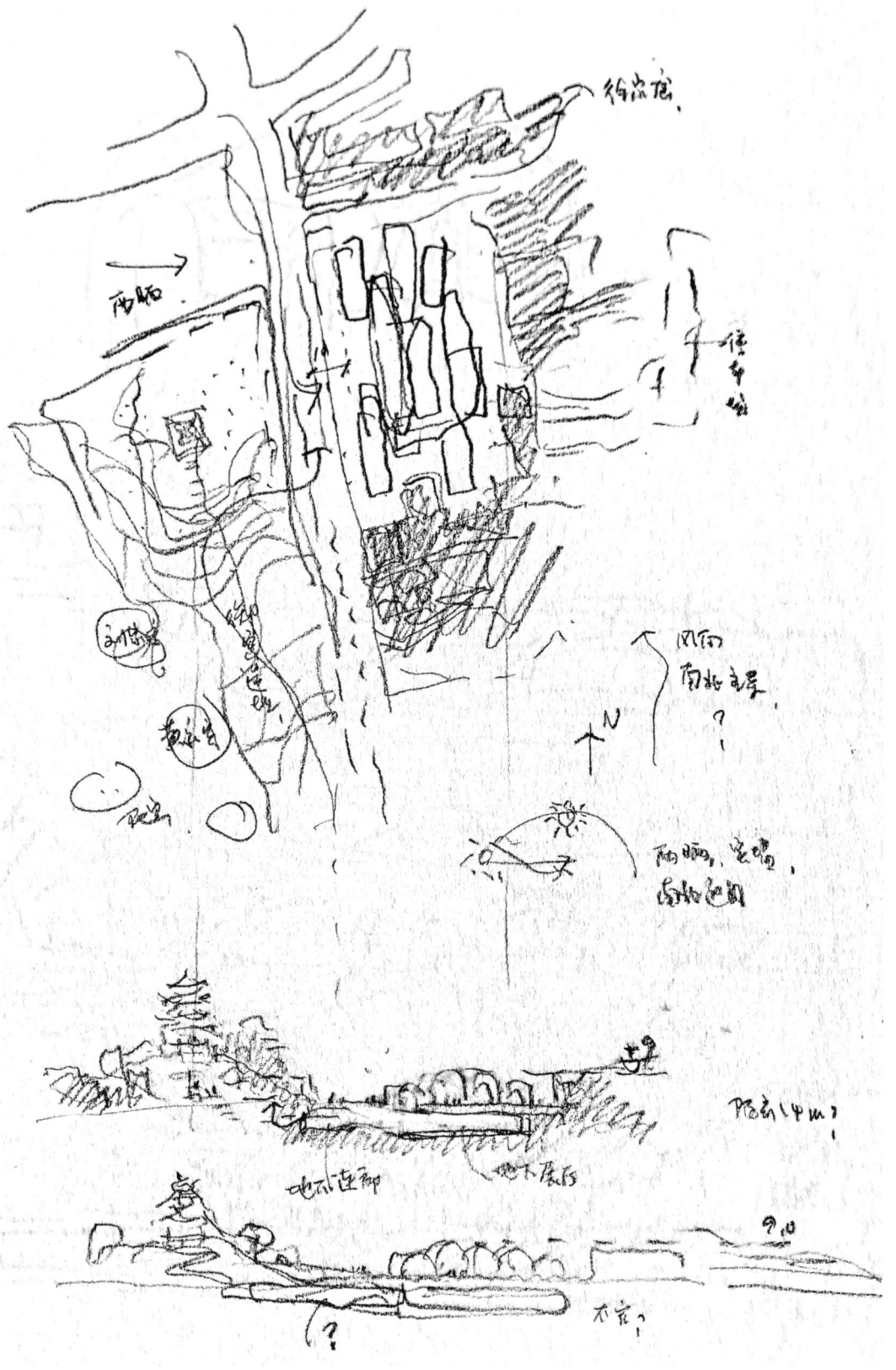

Sketch by Zhu Pei
Pencil on paper
12×9.7 in (30.5×24.6 cm)

Sketch by Zhu Pei (partial sketch)
Pencil on paper
12×9.7 in (30.5×24.6 cm)

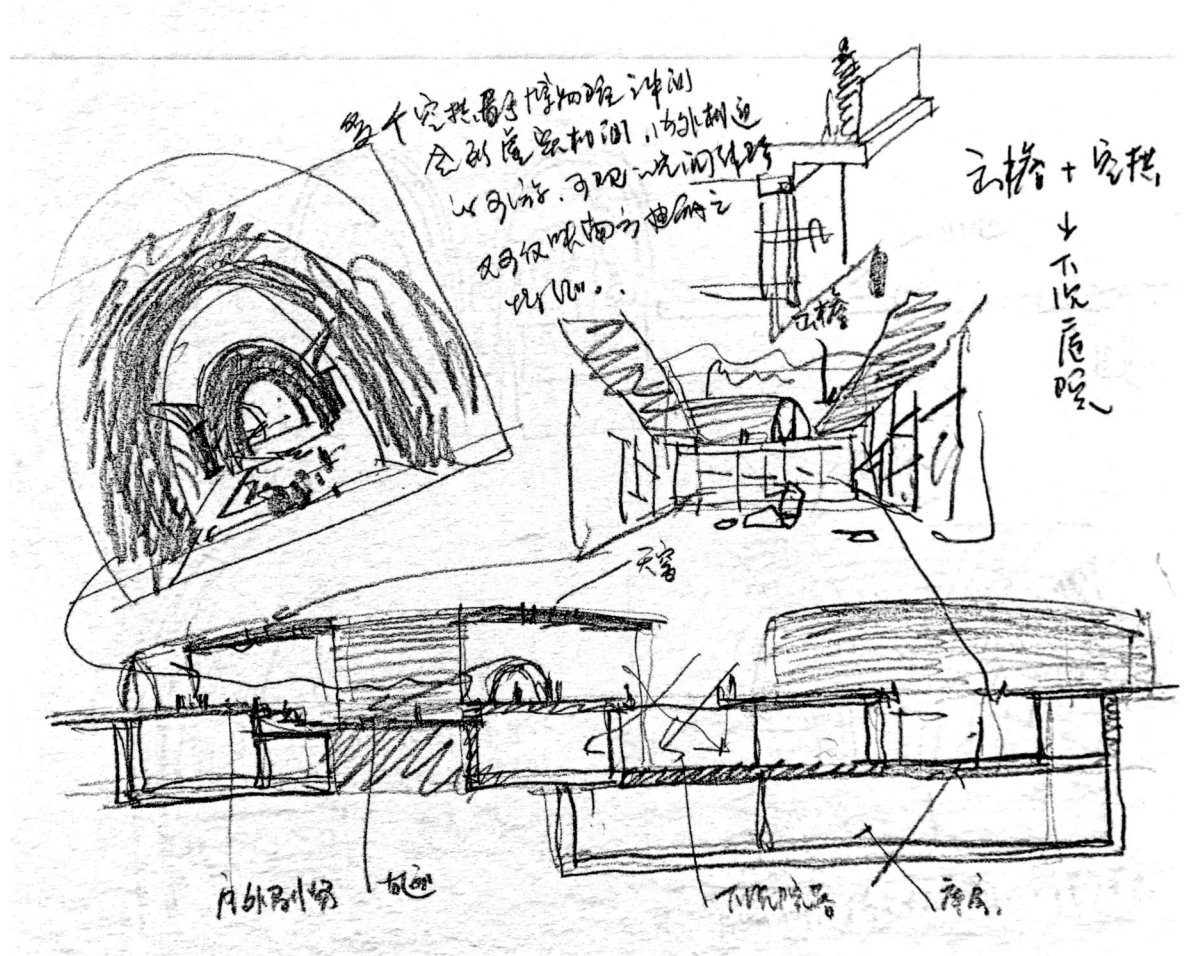

59

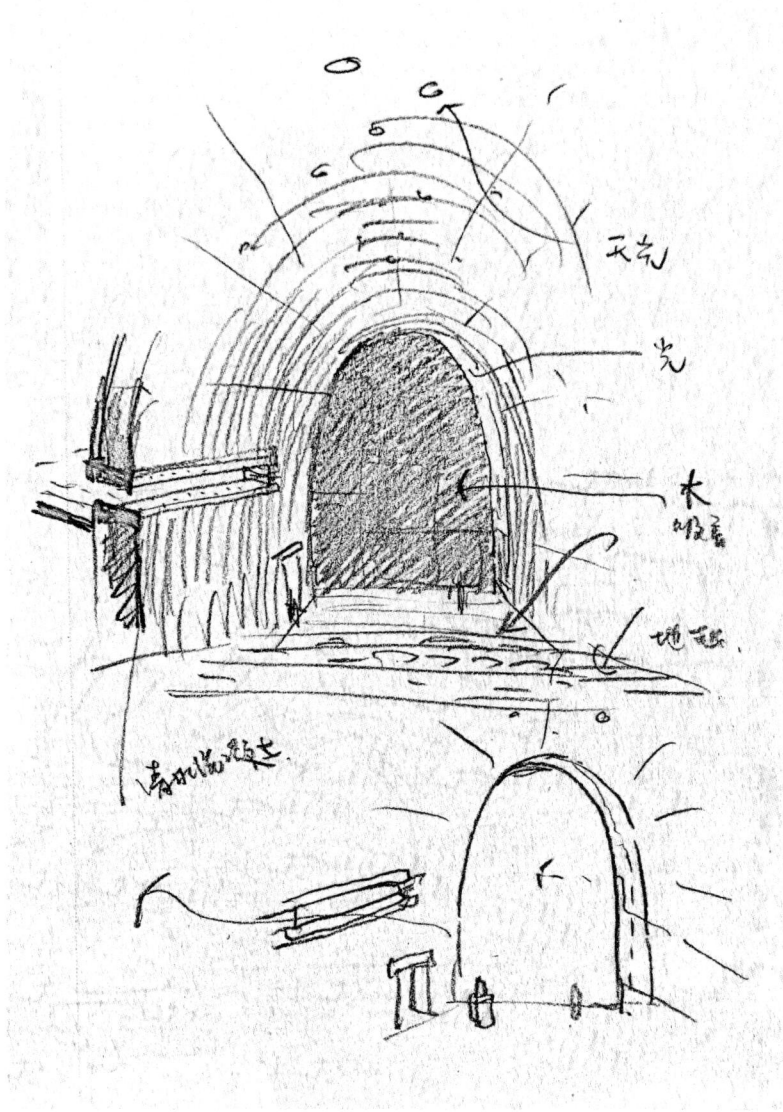

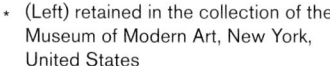

Sketch by Zhu Pei
Pencil on paper
8.5×6.3 in (21.6×15.9 cm)

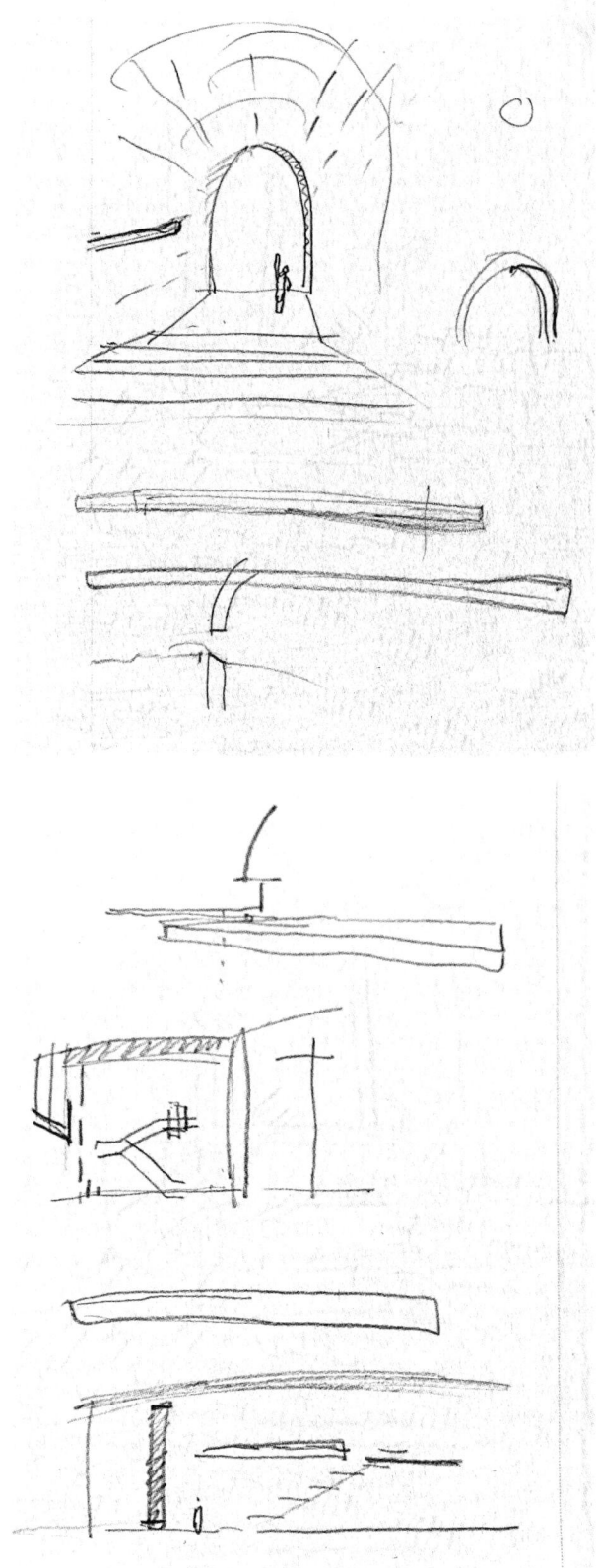

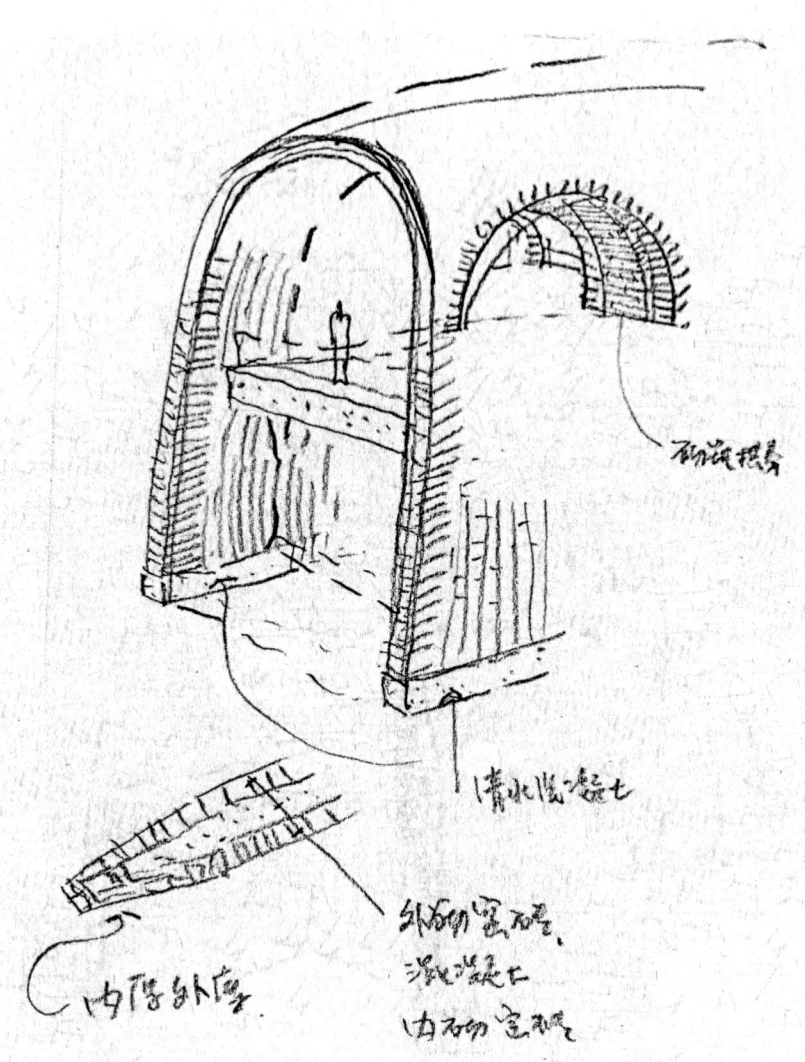

石海相乐

清水混凝土

外砌窑砖，
混凝土
内砌宝砖

内饰外壁

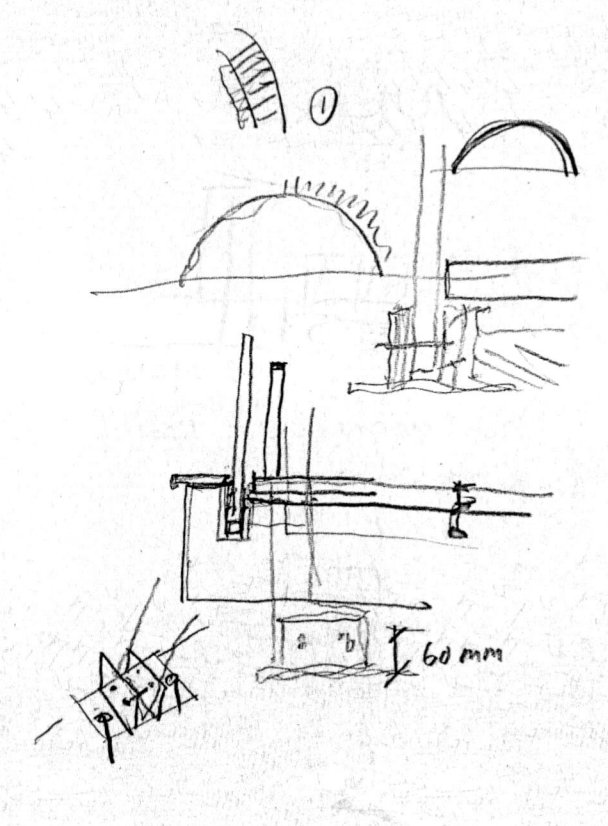

①

60 mm

Concept

The Imperial Kiln Museum is composed of more than a dozen brick vaults of various volumes arranged in a north–south direction. They are a whole, but separated from each other; integrated with the complexity of the context and in the appropriate scale, yet are held with a humble restraint. On the one hand, the scale of the vault structures is close to that of the surrounding traditional brick kilns, carving a smooth transition between the surrounding large-scale factories, residential buildings, and traditional houses. On the other hand, the uneven length, irregular shifting, and incomplete architectural profile of the vaults skillfully compose an organic stitching with the surrounding uneven boundary. The strategy of "incomplete integrity" has often proven to be forward-looking in dealing with the complex, ever-changing, and unpredictable regeneration of historical districts. During the construction of the museum—soon after it begin, in fact—new archaeological sites in the area were discovered and excavated. While the integration of the site with the museum building increases the archaeological and anthropological characteristics of the museum, it also proves that the strategy of small-scale volumes and incomplete integrity can be applied flexibly in the complex environment of the historic district. Through the spatial coordination of the vaults, the newly discovered ruins were weaved into the internal space of the museum.

With hot and rainy summers being a significant climatic condition in Jingdezhen, one of the most important ideas behind the design was to create a porous, sponge-like building that maximizes natural ventilation, while extending shelter from the sun and rain without the need for air conditioning during summer. Both ends of the long axis of each vault of the museum complex are open. In particular, these open, semi-outdoor vaults, and relatively closed indoor vaults, are staggered with each other, alternating the solid and void, shaping the porous characteristics of the museum similar to a "sponge architecture." The long axis of the vault is arranged along the north–south direction. The vault not only blocks the sunlight on the west side, but also provides sun shading and shelter from the rain in a design that also turns each vault into a windy tunnel, allowing cool breezes to pass through, especially to capture the dominant north–south wind direction during summer. In the five sunken courtyards of varying sizes and scales, bamboos are planted to create a poetic space, where the underground level is illuminated by natural light. This presents as a typical Jiangxi Province feature and creates the chimney effect experienced in local vertical courtyards, which helps to enhance natural ventilation. On a hot summer day, when visitors step into the museum, they will always feel a cool breeze. The whole building complex resembles an installation composed of wind, air, and shadow, intelligently blending and coexisting with nature.

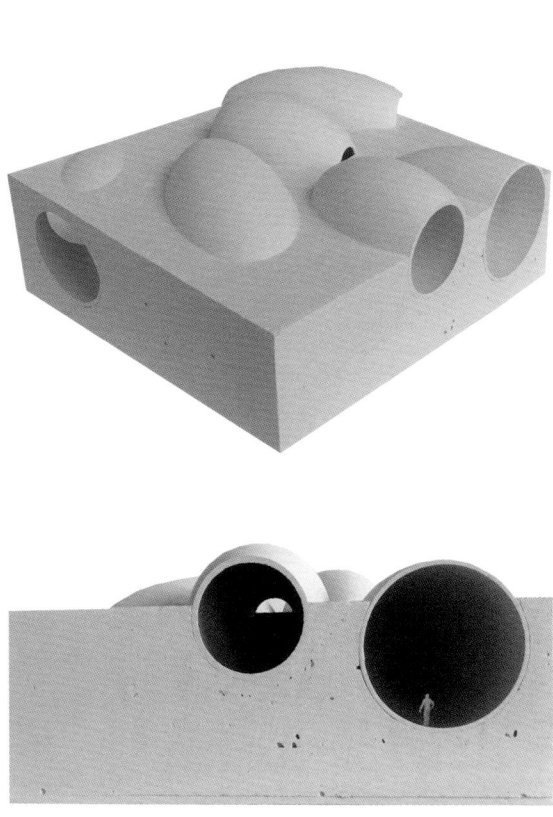

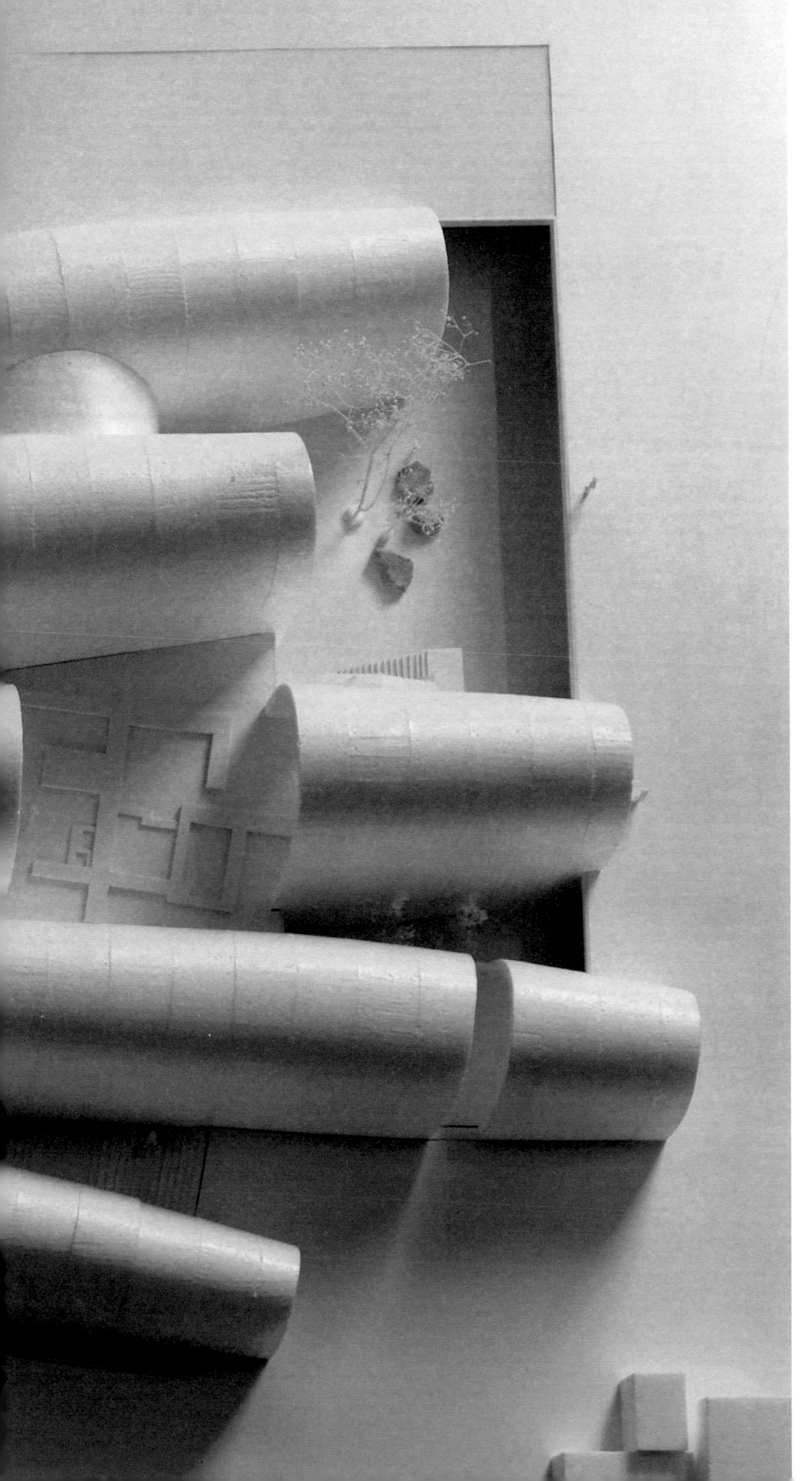

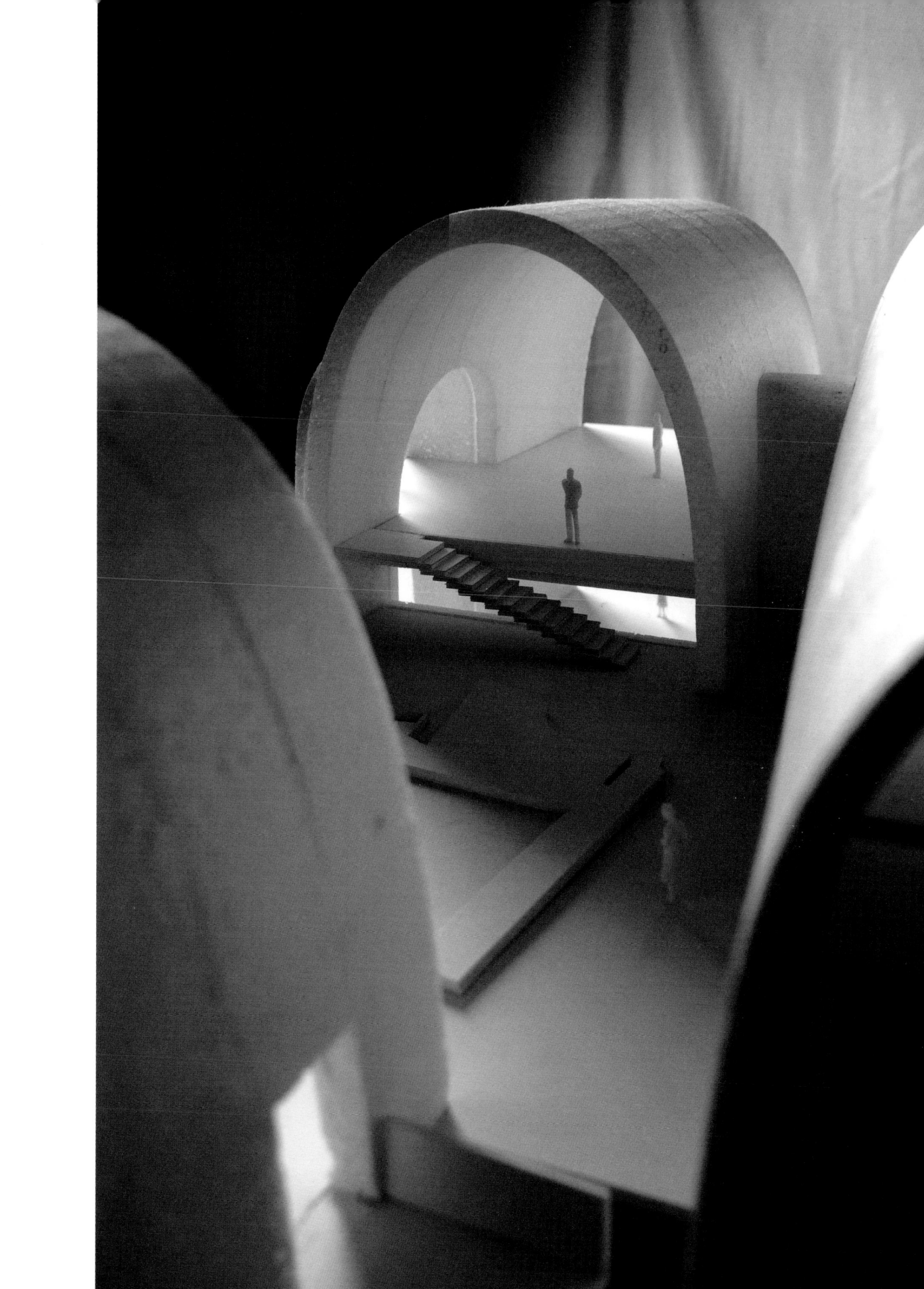

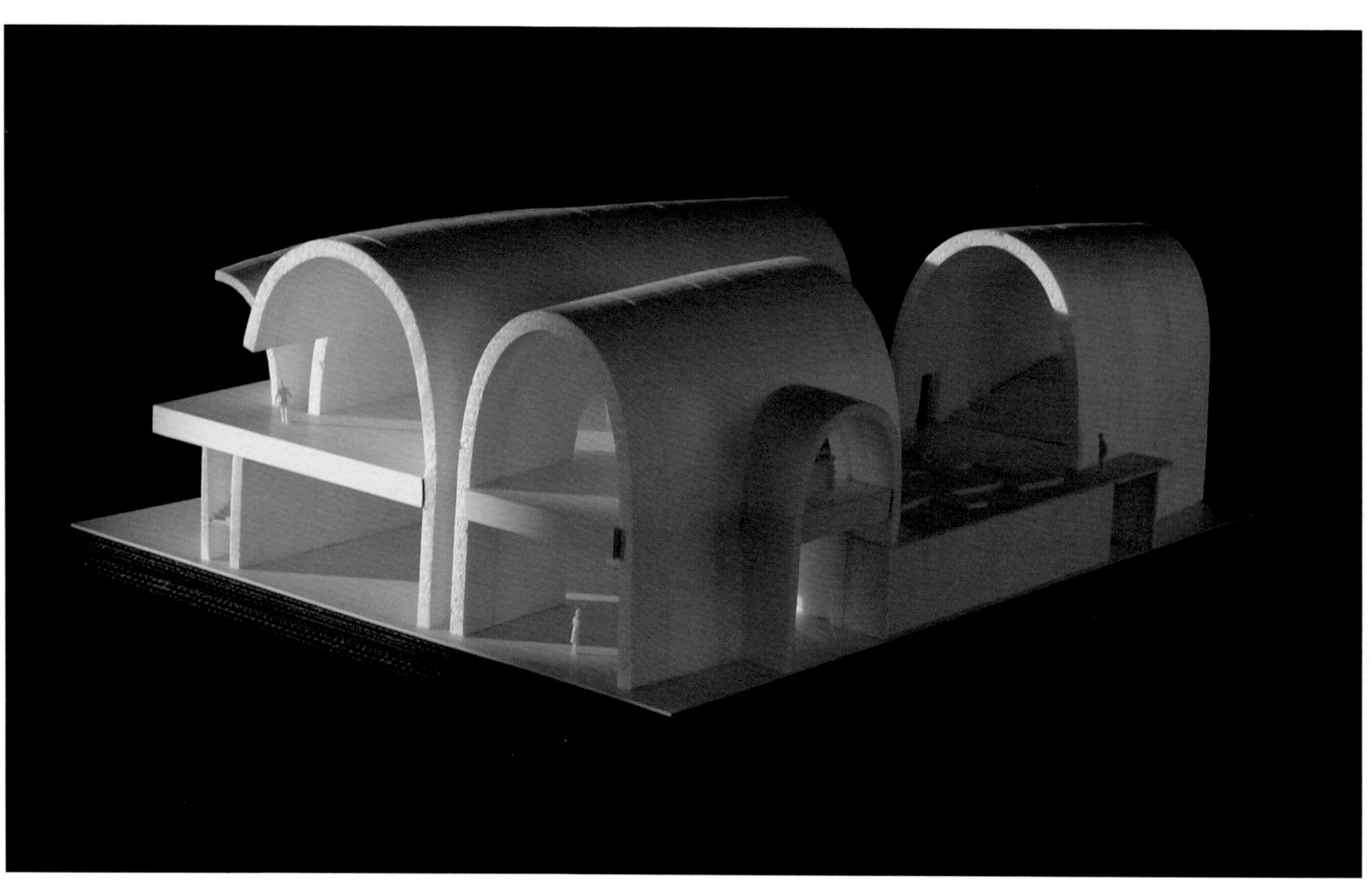

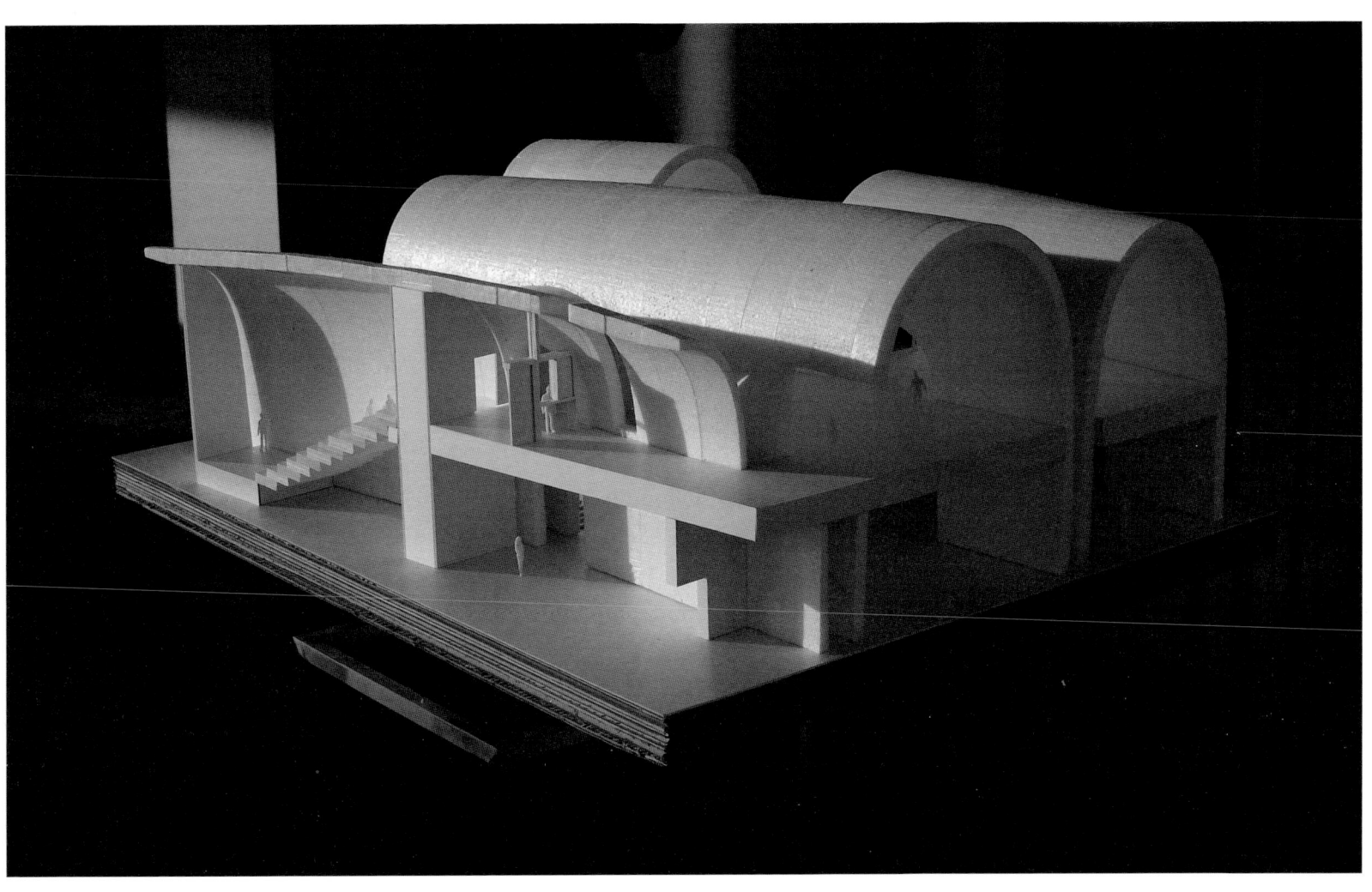

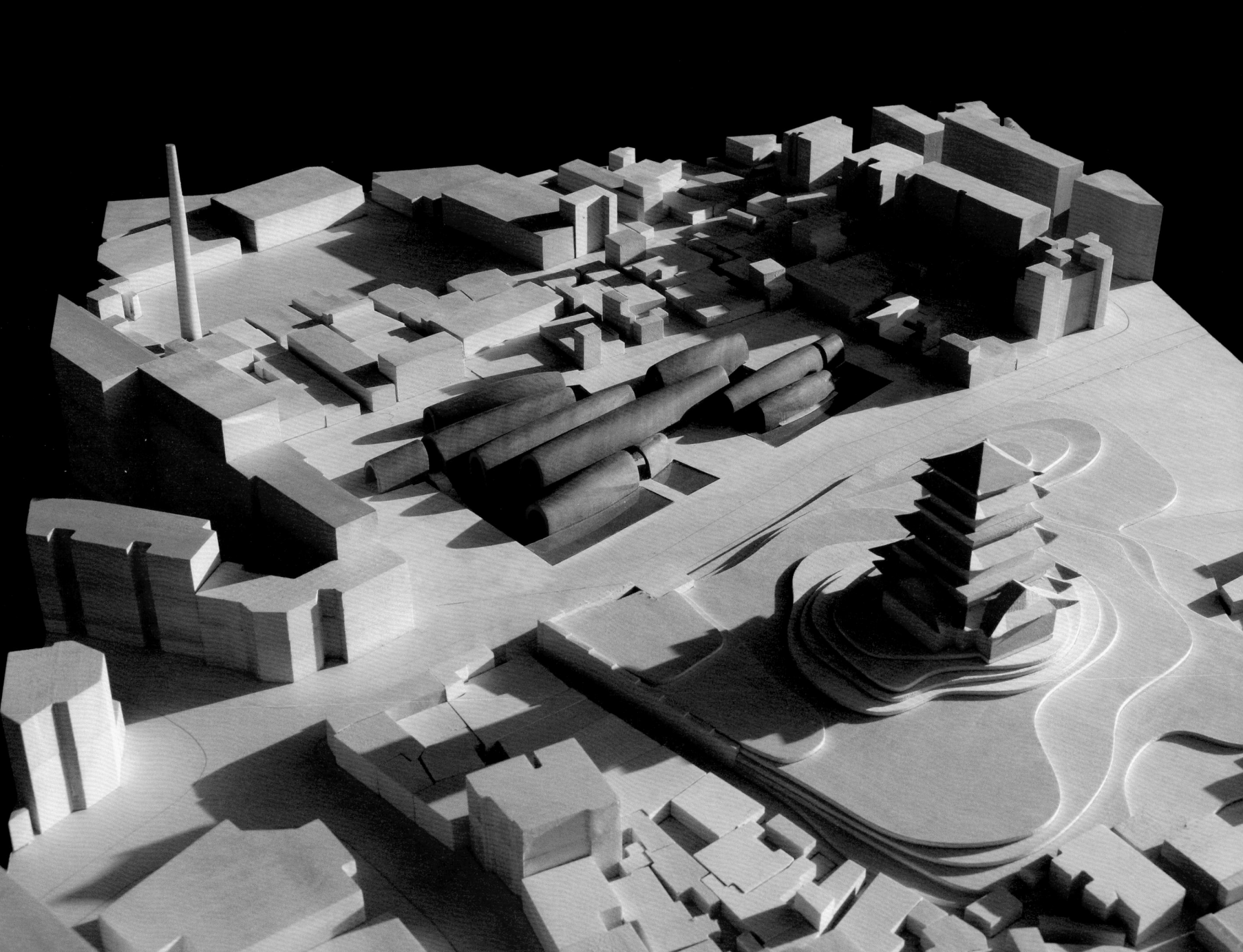

Wood
13.3×36.5×33.5 in
(33.7×92.7×85.1 cm)

78

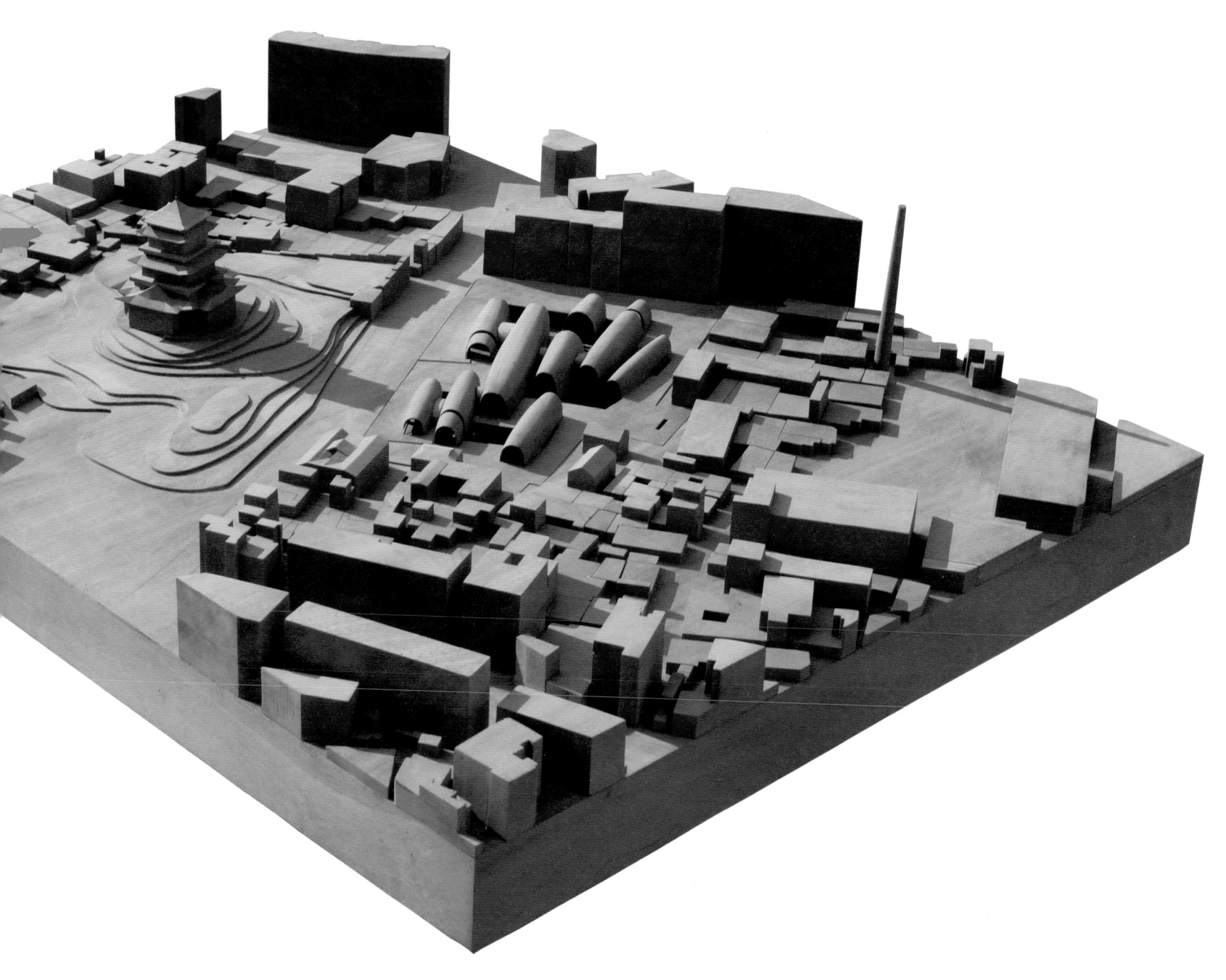

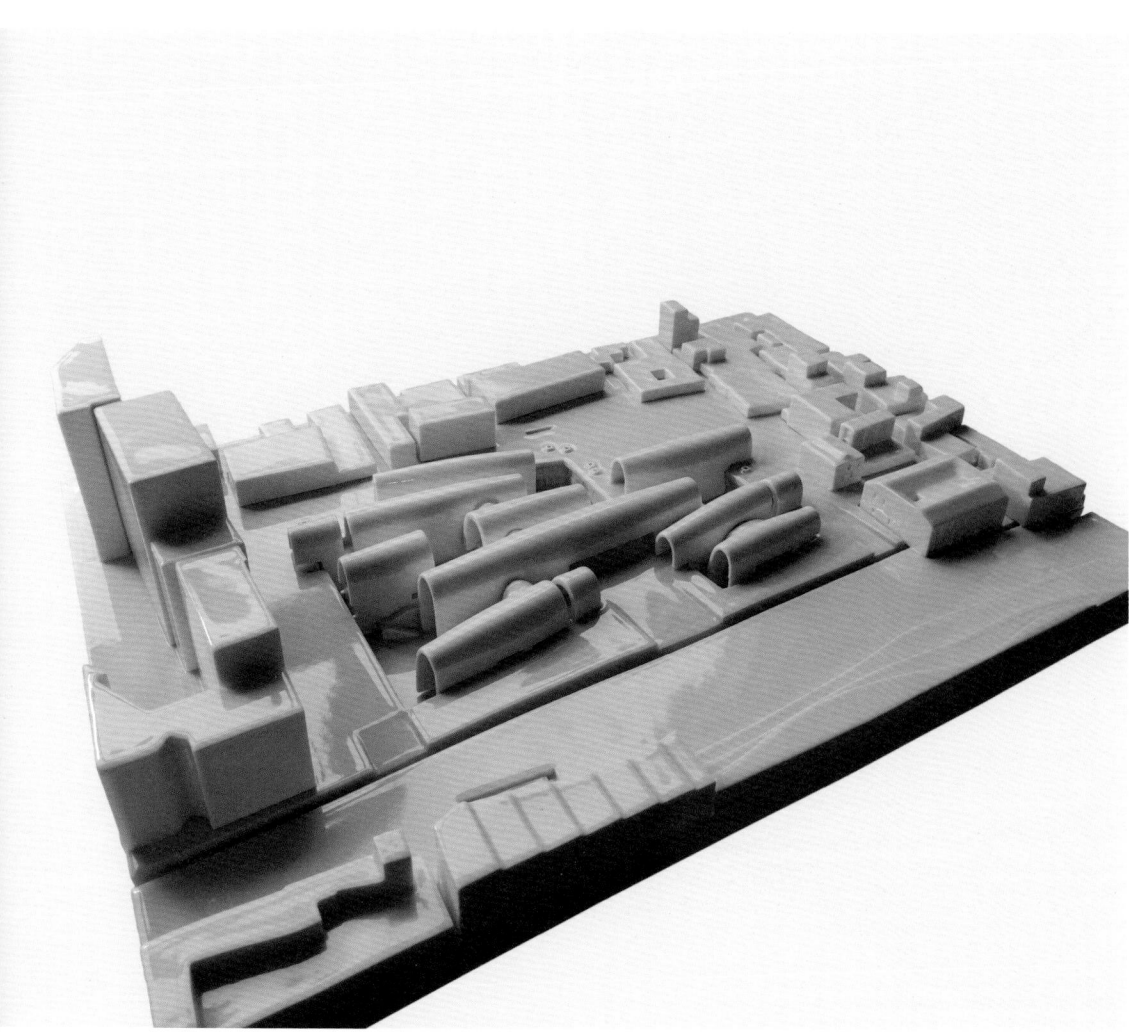

Porcelain
4.9×25.5×18 in (12.4×64.8×45.7 cm)

Site plan

1   Longzhu Pavilion
2   Imperial Kiln Museum
3   New residential area developed in the 1990s
4   Jianguo Porcelain Factory built in the 1950s
5   Historical neighborhood
6   Liujiayao Kiln ruins
7   Huang Laoda Kiln ruins
8   Civilian kiln ruins from the Ming dynasty
9   Imperial Kiln ruins
10   Xujiayao Kiln ruins

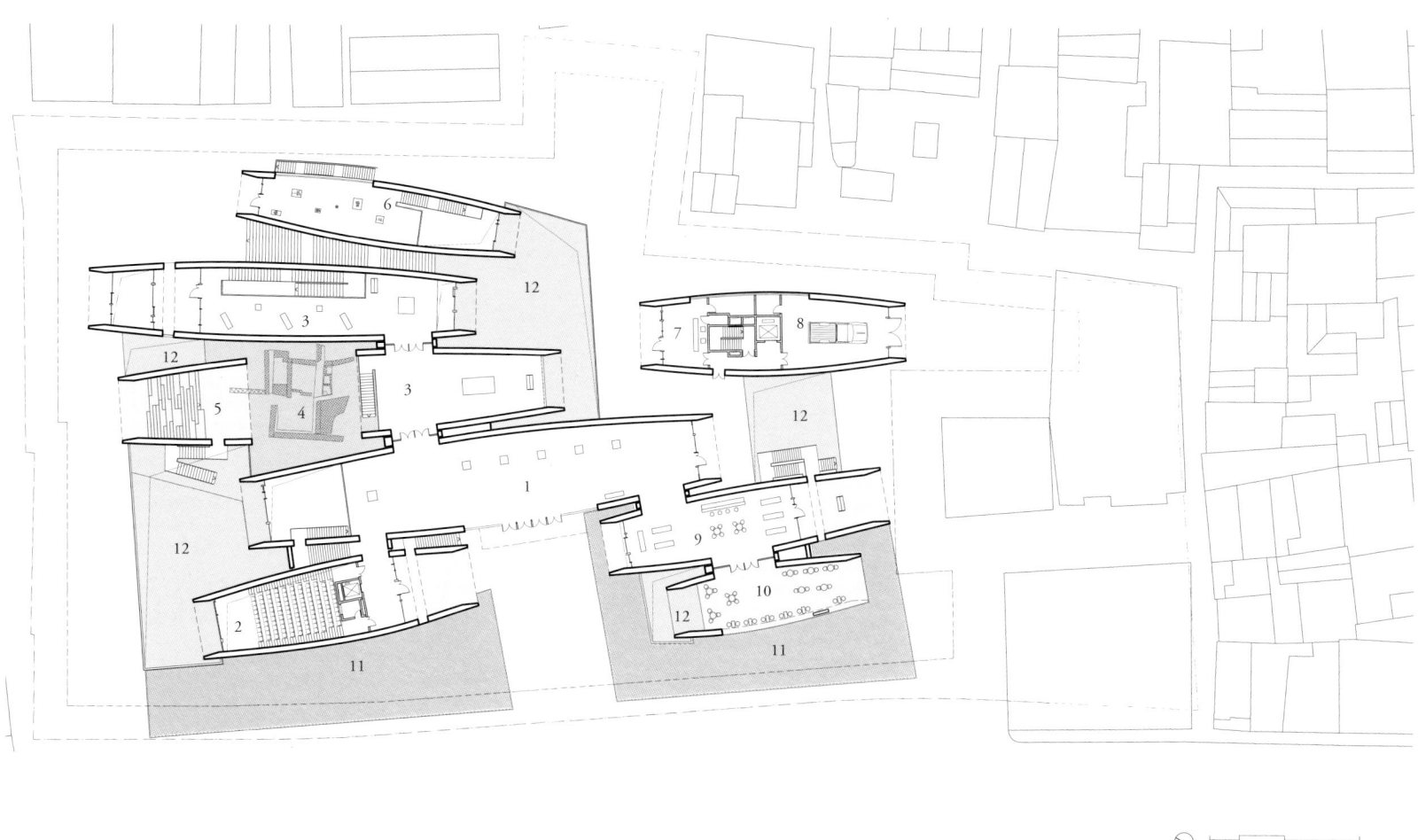

Ground-floor plan

1	Lobby/Foyer	5	Amphitheater	9	Bookstore and café
2	Auditorium	6	Temporary exhibition	10	Tearoom
3	Permanent exhibition	7	Office lobby	11	Pool
4	Civilian kiln ruins from the Ming dynasty	8	Loading dock	12	Sunken courtyard

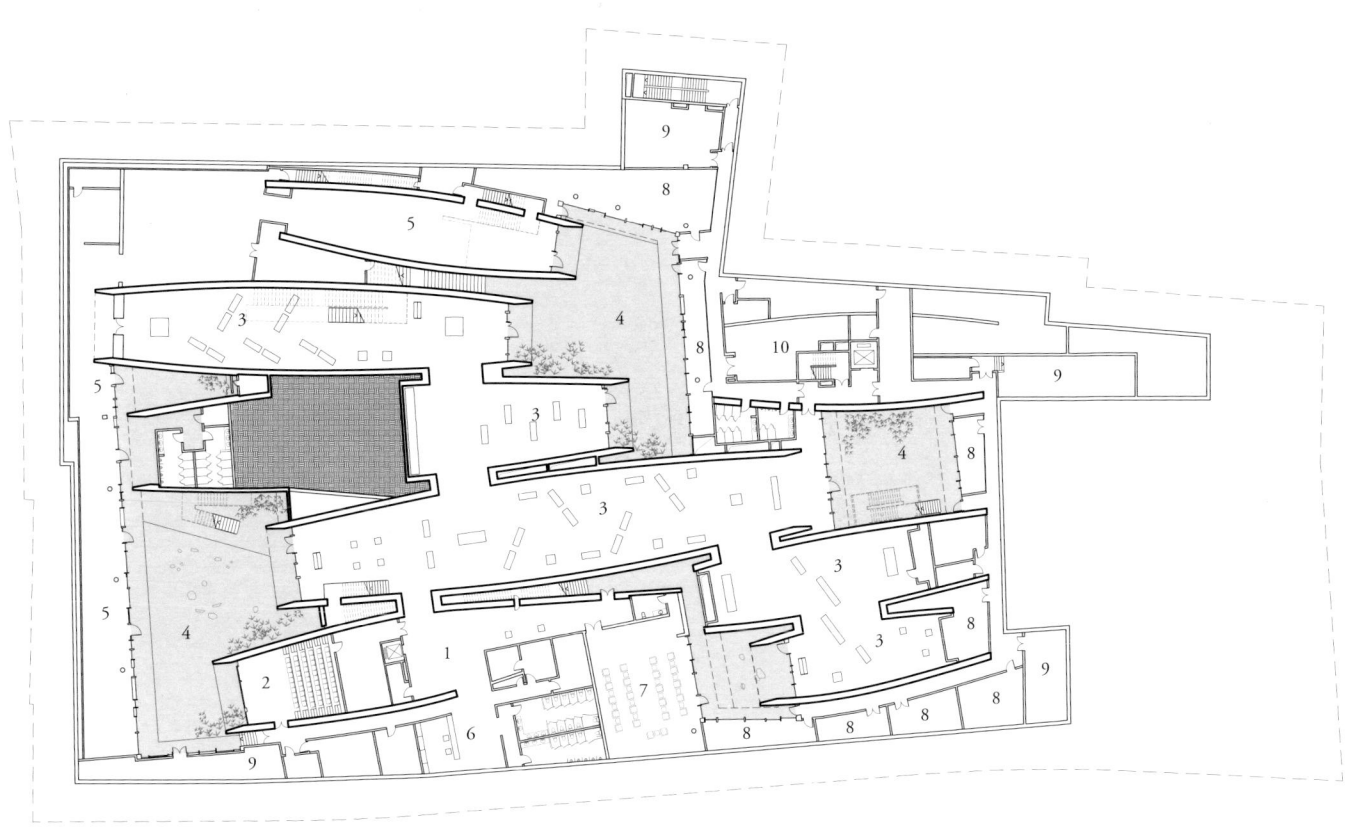

Underground-floor plan

1 Foyer
2 Auditorium
3 Permanent exhibition
4 Sunken courtyard

5 Temporary exhibition
6 Coat check
7 Multifunction hall
8 Restoration room

9 Mechanical room
10 Storage

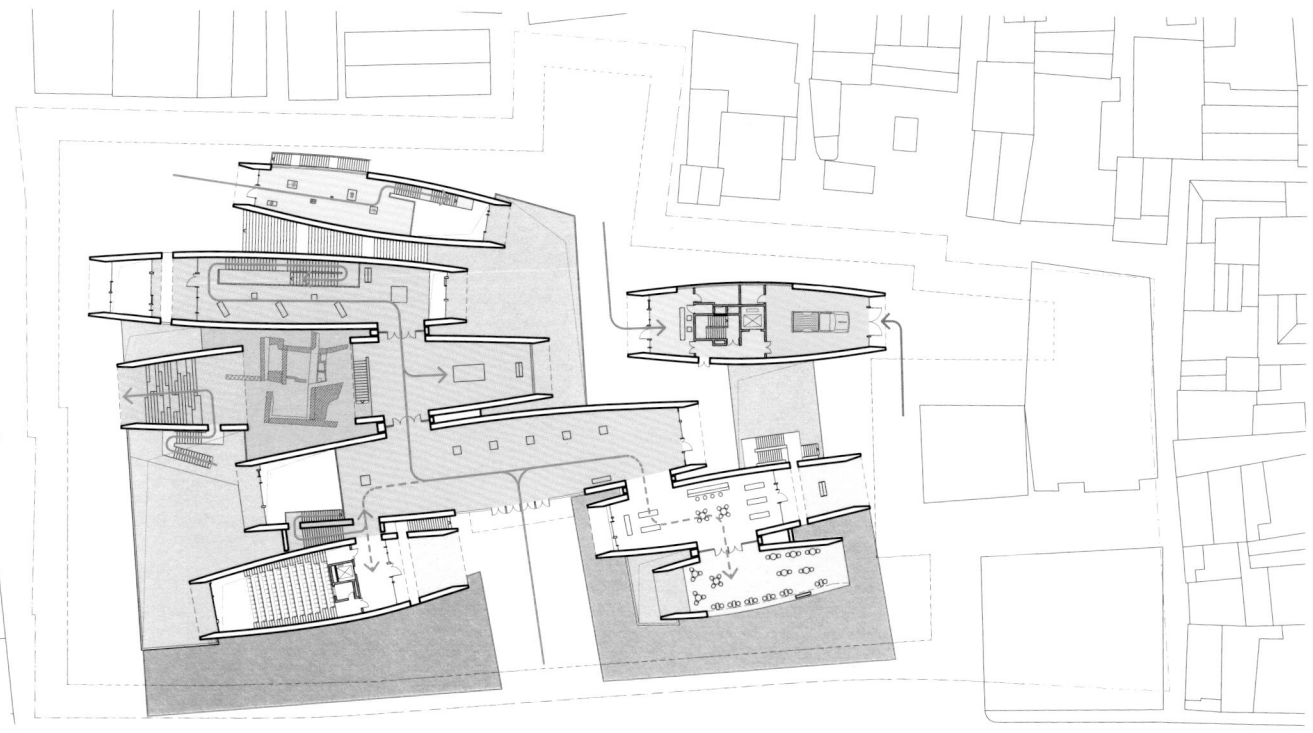

Ground-floor plan: circulation analysis

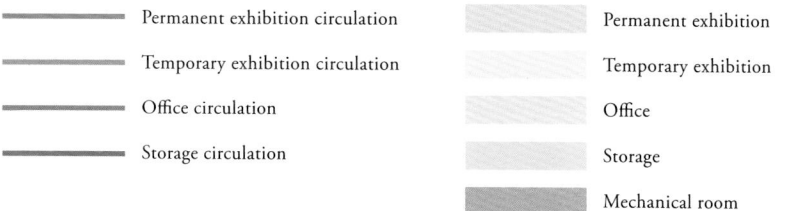

————— Permanent exhibition circulation	▨ Permanent exhibition
————— Temporary exhibition circulation	▨ Temporary exhibition
————— Office circulation	▨ Office
————— Storage circulation	▨ Storage
	▨ Mechanical room

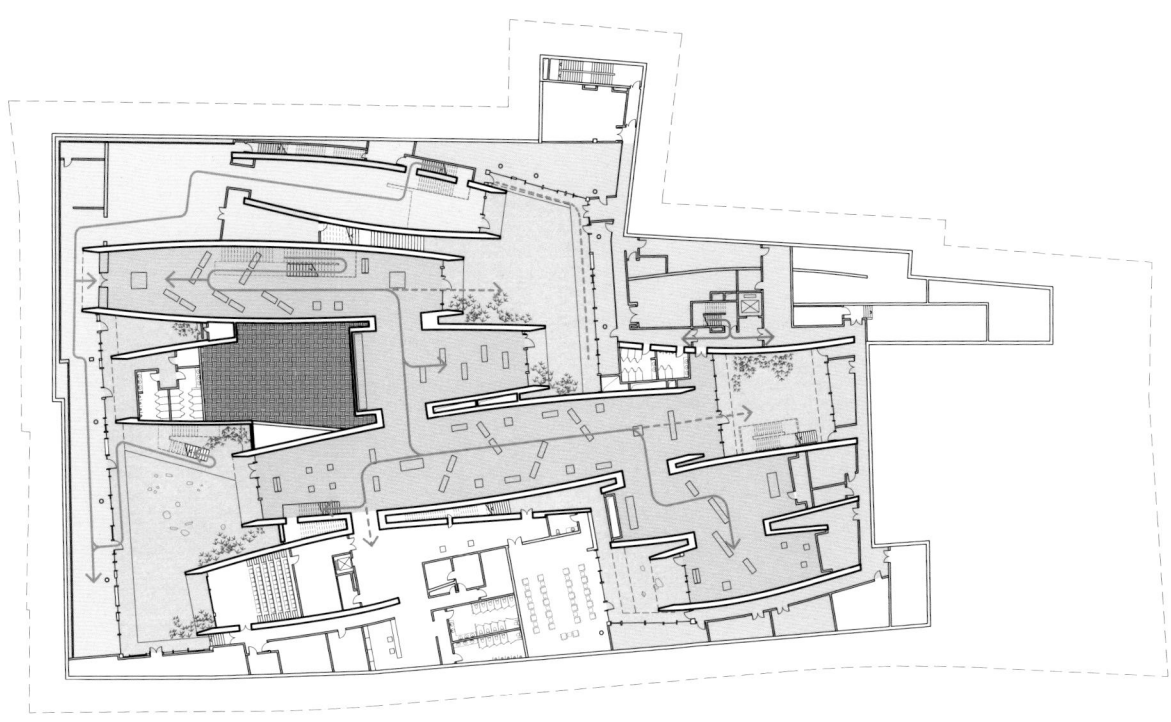

Underground-floor plan: circulation analysis

Second underground-floor plan: circulation analysis

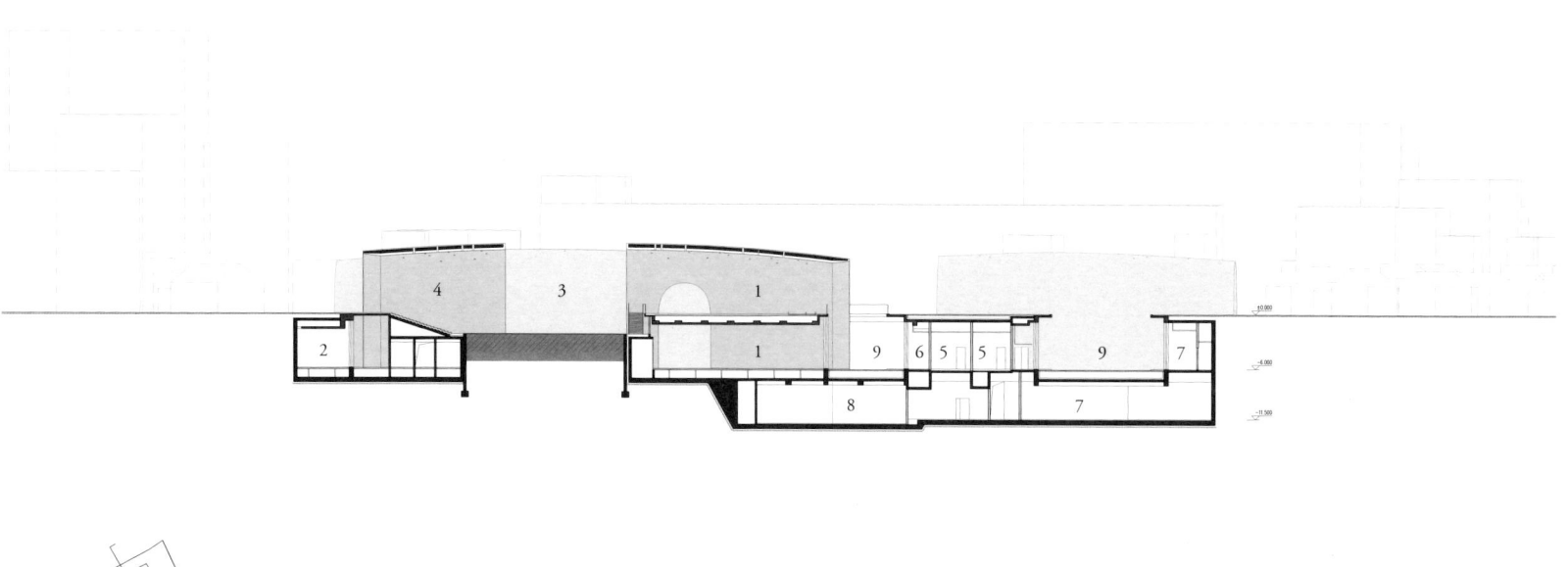

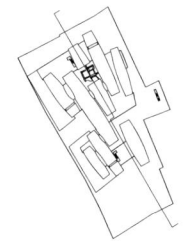

Section 1

1	Permanent exhibition	5	Restroom	9	Sunken courtyard
2	Temporary exhibition	6	Restoration room		
3	Civilian kiln ruins from the Ming dynasty	7	Storage		
4	Amphitheater	8	Air-conditioning facilities room		

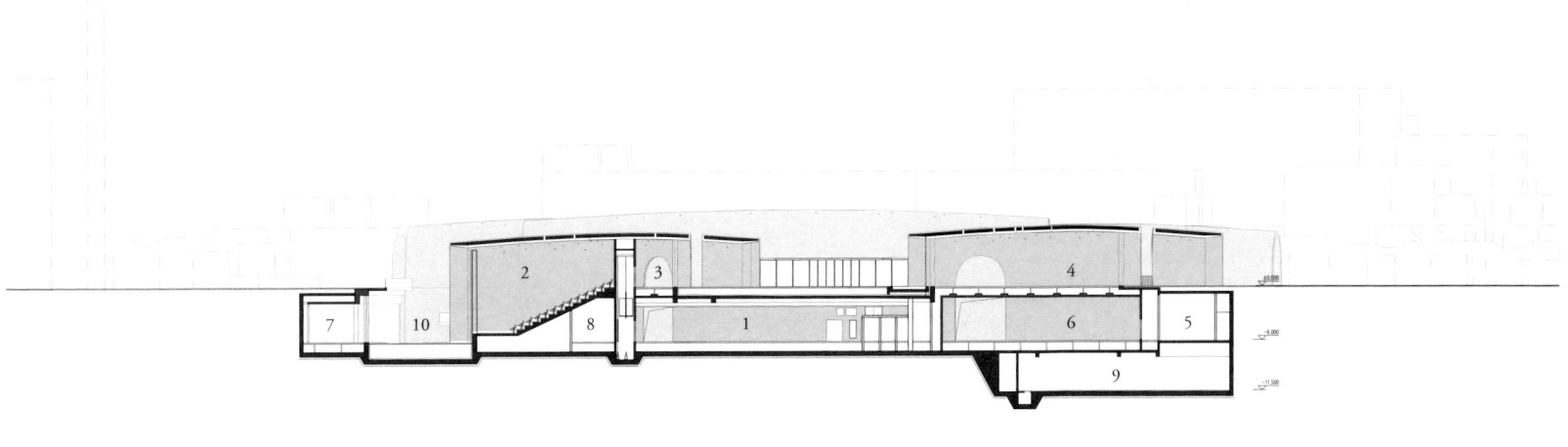

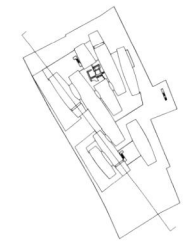

Section 2

1	Foyer	5	Mechanical room	9	Storage
2	Auditorium	6	Permanent exhibition	10	Sunken courtyard
3	Lobby of auditorium	7	Temporary exhibition		
4	Bookstore and café	8	Air-conditioning facilities room		

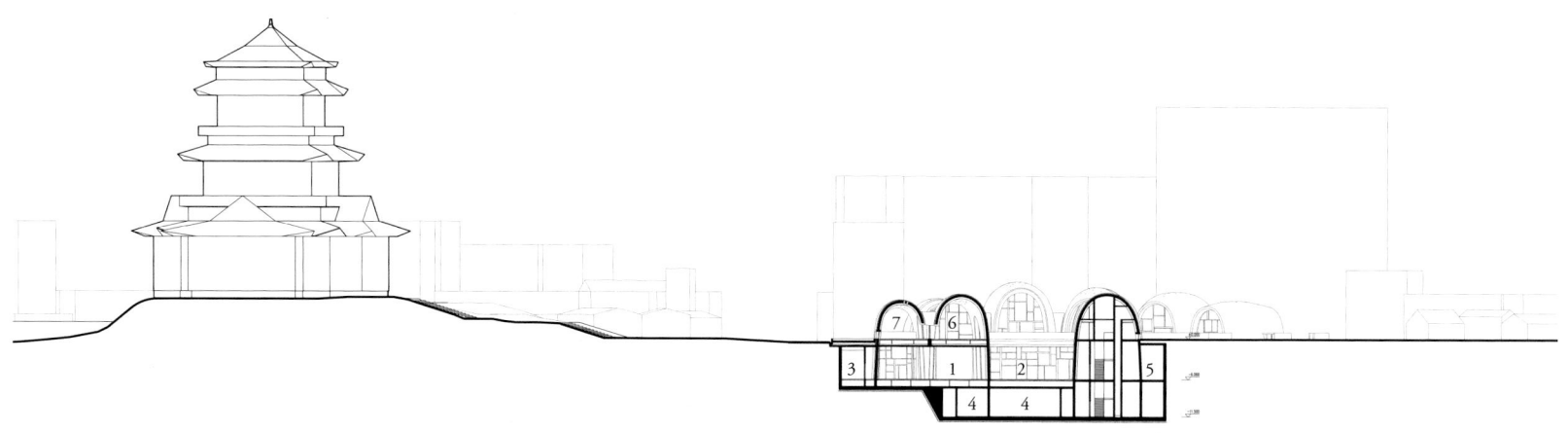

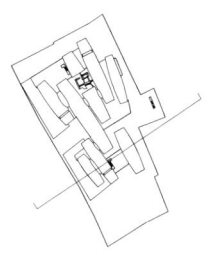

Section 3

1   Permanent exhibition
2   Sunken courtyard
3   Restoration room
4   Storage
5   Mechanical room
6   Bookstore and café
7   Tearoom

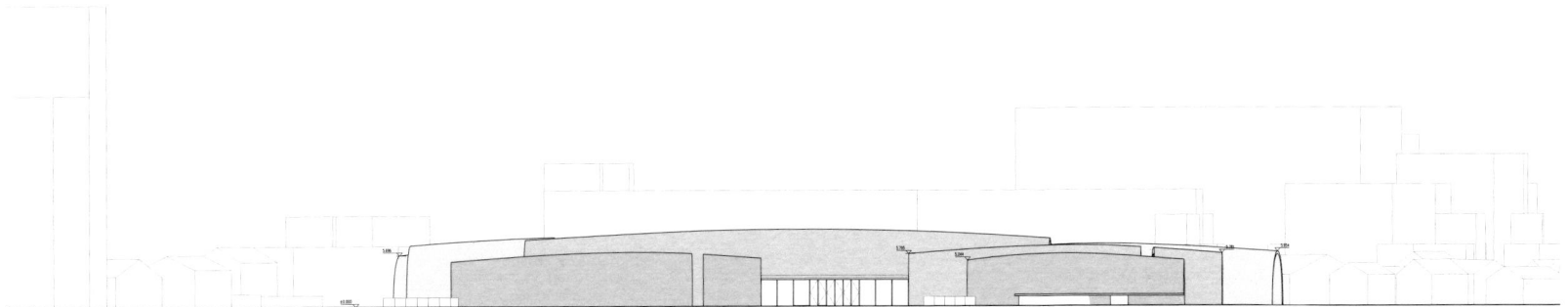

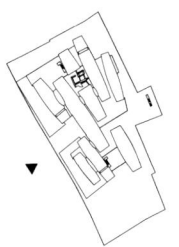

West elevation

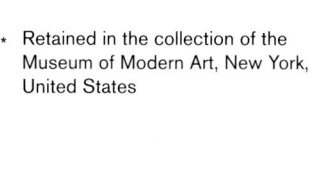

Axonometric drawing: aerial view of the museum and surroundings

Tectonic

Determining how to create a poetic and artistic contemporary translation of the structural form of the traditional brick kiln vault from the perspective of tectonics was the key to the architectural form of the Imperial Kiln Museum. First, the museum took the traditional brick kiln as a prototype, abstracting and simplifying the pure brick vault structure into a simple double-curved vault architectural form. The structural section of each vault is similar to a sandwich; the inner and outer layers of bricks wrap the reinforced-concrete vault structure in the middle, and the concrete vault in the middle is the main structure of the building that resists lateral force during earthquakes. The inner and outer layers of structures are built with a mixture of new and old kiln bricks. This composite vault structure system composed of brick and concrete is similar to the construction system of the ancient Roman arch: brick or stone + concrete vault + brick or stone. Second, where most traditional brick kilns are standalone and independent structures, and protected by wooden kiln sheds, the Imperial Kiln Museum appears in the form of a pure vault group combination: more than a dozen main vaults are arranged north–south on their long axis and interspersed with several small vault structures from east to west, weaving the overall structural system of the museum. From the section, the vault structure vertically spans two floors, and the mezzanine adopts a hollow equipment interlayer. The mezzanine is a U-shaped fair-faced concrete structure, which is the transverse support structure of the vault structure. Its top surface features concrete corrugated steel plates; granite bluestone slabs wrap the first floor; and the bottom surface is exposed fair-faced concrete, which forms the ceiling of the underground exhibition space.

In Jingdezhen, there is a tradition that has lasted for nearly a thousand years, which is the reusing old kiln bricks. When a traditional brick kiln has been firing for a year, or two, at the most, the kiln bricks would by then have completed their life cycle, taking on decaying heat storage properties.

Hence, they would be replaced by new bricks. These old bricks with their "kiln sweat" (a crystalline compound of wood ash and clay minerals vaporized through years of ceramic firing) are mixed with new bricks to become the main construction material in the building of local residential houses. This tradition continues to this day. The same tradition of mixing old and new bricks has also been inherited by the Imperial Kiln Museum; sometimes, the new bricks are mixed with a large amount of sand from crushed saggers (refractory baked clay boxes used to hold finer ceramics during firing). The museum adopts a minimalistic material palette, with concrete, brick, and wood being the three main materials. Brick and concrete are used together to construct the architraves; the floor slabs, cross-over beams, and staircases are constructed in concrete; and wood is used as the main mullion structure for the glass curtain wall.

Recycled kiln bricks used in residential constructions

An archaeological excavation site

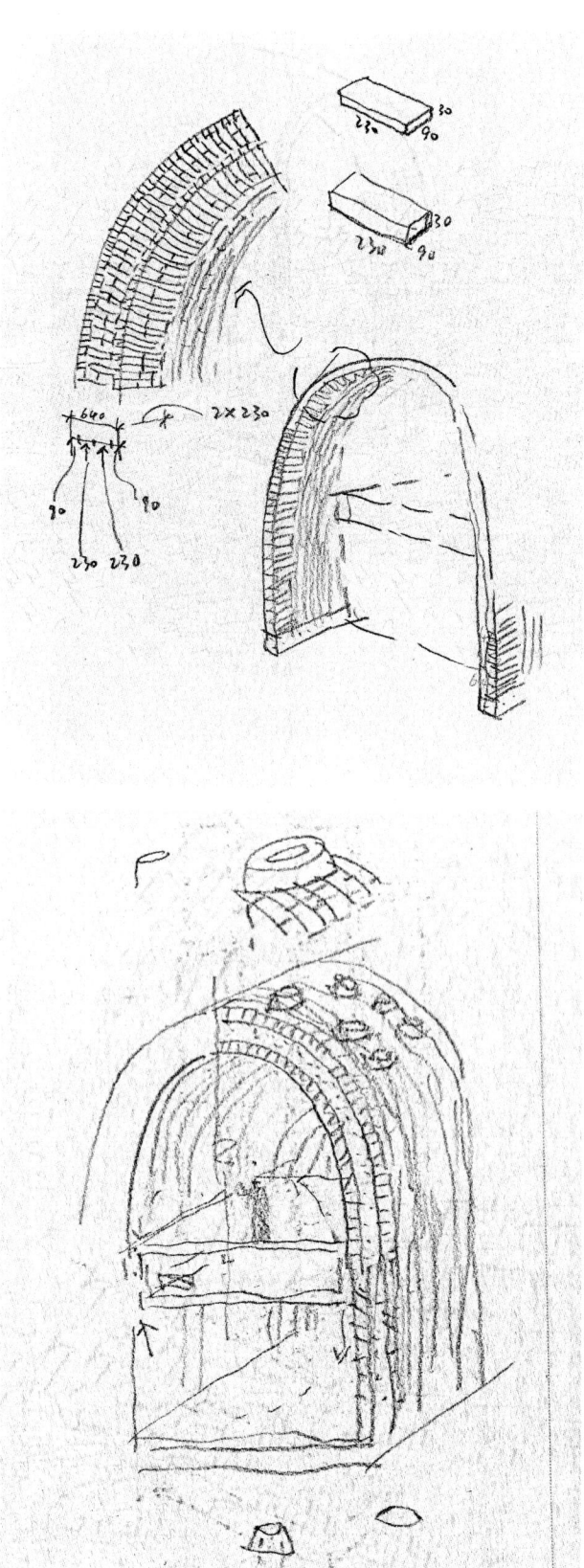

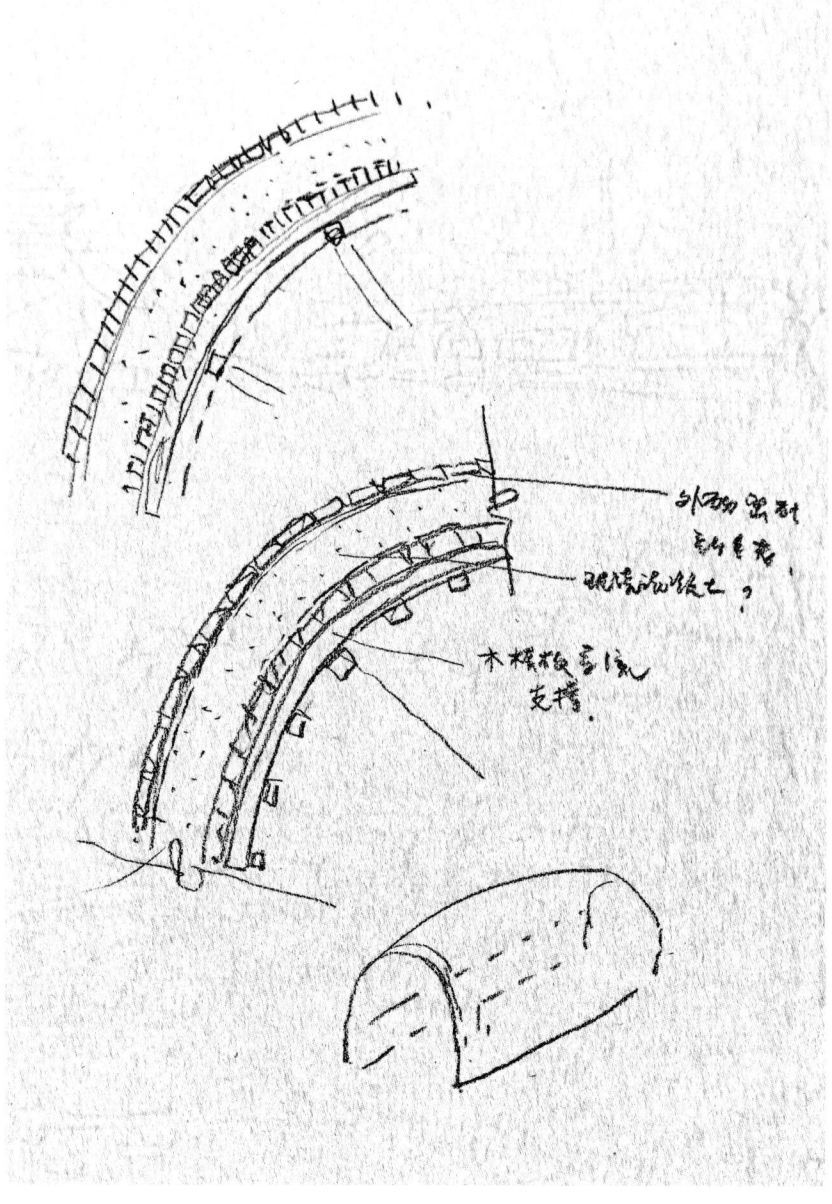

外面的 混凝土
封毛 ?

现浇混凝土 ?

木模板或充气
支撑.

1. this museum is inspired by
Local historical kiln,

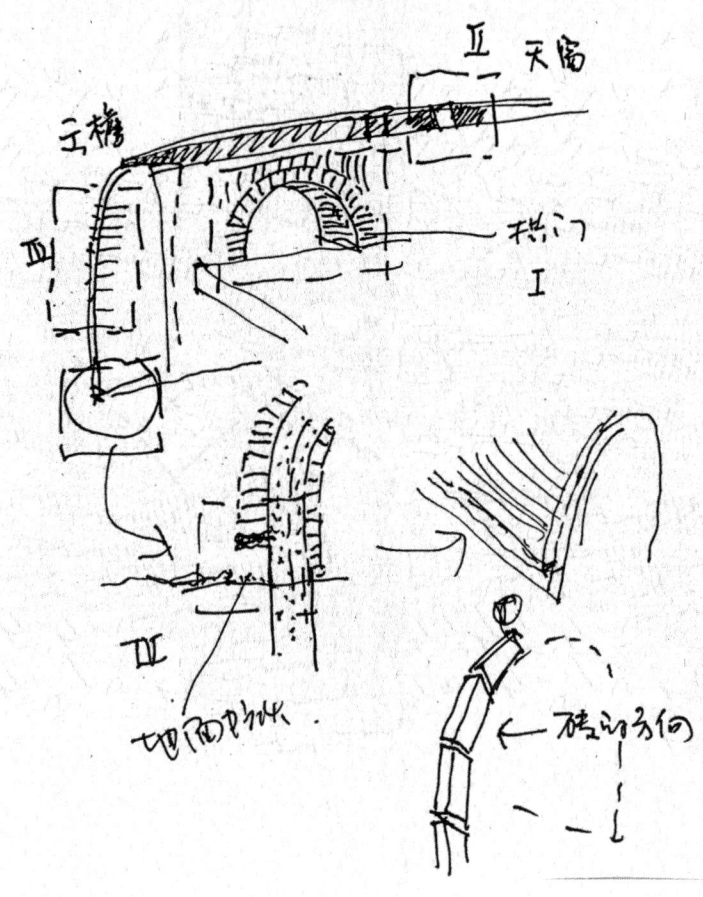

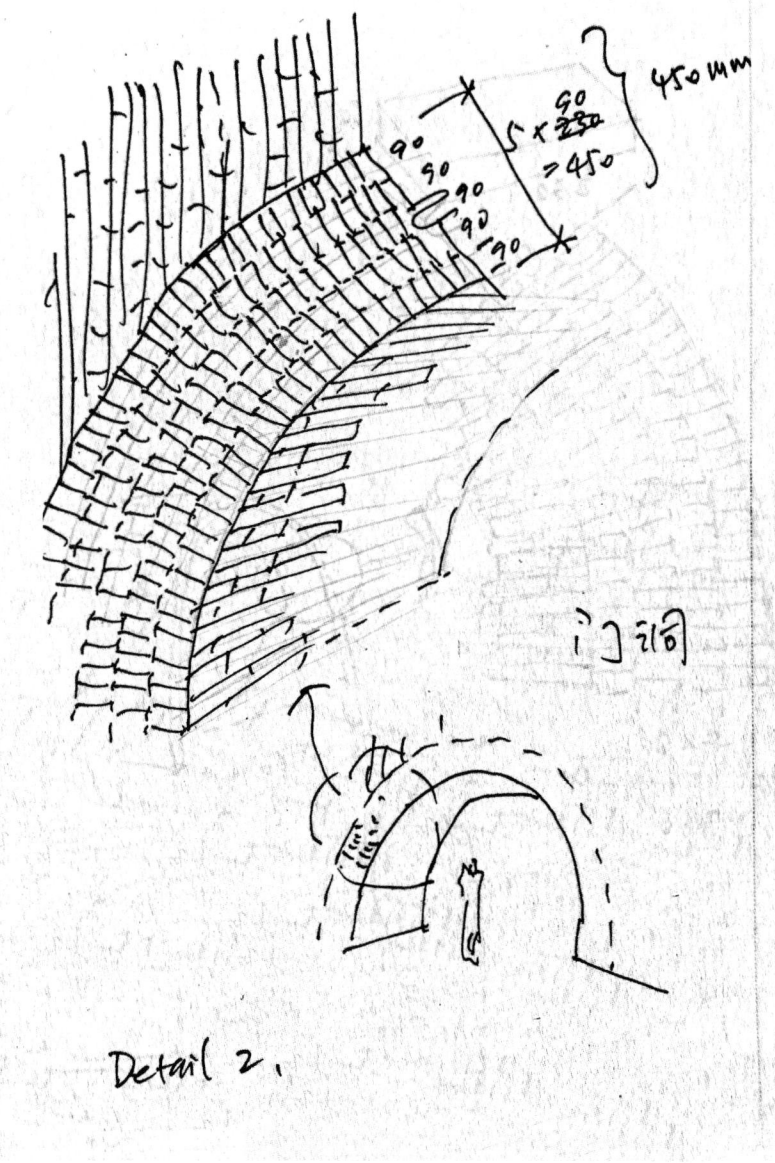

450 mm

门洞

Detail 2.

* (Right) retained in the collection of
the Museum of Modern Art, New York,
United States

Sketch by Zhu Pei
Marker on paper
8.5×6.3 in (21.6×15.9 cm)

Detail A: vertical section (opposite page)

1 Fair-faced concrete lintel of 300 mm height
40-mm-wide stainless-steel door frame
8+1.52PVB+8 extra clear tempered laminated glass

2 Water
50 mm black pebble with grain size 50–70 mm
600×600×30 mm gray granite
20 mm 1:3 cement mortar binding layer
150 mm reinforced-concrete pool

3 6+1.52PVB+6 tempered laminated glass panel

4 90×40 mm aluminum C-profile framing suspended by tie rods
12 mm flame-retardant panel
12 mm moisture-resistant gypsum board
White oak veneer

5 40 mm granite floor
60 mm 1:3 dry, hard cement mortar bonding layer
Steel corrugated sheet and 100 mm concrete pouring
Equipment interlayer
10 mm 1:2 cement mortar protective layer
One 1.5 mm waterproof mortar, cement-based penetrating crystalline
P6 impermeable reinforced-concrete floor

6 80 mm granite floor
30 mm 1:3 dry, hard cement mortar bonding layer
100 mm C15 plain concrete cushion
Plain soil compaction
200 g/m^3 non-woven filter layer
Concave-convex drainage board
70 mm C20 fine stone concrete protective layer
0.4 mm polyethylene plastic film insulation
4+3 mm SBS-modified bituminous waterproofing membrane
20 mm cement mortar leveling layer
(The thinnest part is) 40 mm aerated fragmented concrete topping forming slop
P6 impermeable reinforced-concrete floor

7 Kiln brick horizontal masonry; specification: 230×30×60 mm
30 mm 1:2 cement mortar
One 1.5 mm waterproof mortar, cement-based penetrating crystalline
P6 impermeable reinforced-concrete vault structure, ends thinning
30 mm 1:2 cement mortar
Kiln brick horizontal masonry; specification: 230×30×60 mm

8 New and reclaimed kiln brick masonry; specification: 230×30×60 mm
30 mm 1:2 cement mortar
One 1.5 mm waterproof mortar, cement-based penetrating crystalline
P6 impermeable reinforced-concrete vault structure
60 mm dry, hard insulation rock wool board
30 mm 1:2 cement mortar
Kiln brick masonry; specification: 230×30×60 mm

9 40 mm granite floor
60 mm 1:3 dry, hard cement mortar bonding layer
Steel corrugated sheet and 100 mm concrete pouring
Equipment interlayer
10 mm 1:2 cement mortar protective layer
One 1.5 mm waterproof mortar, cement-based penetrating crystalline
Reinforced-concrete floor with fair-faced concrete bottom

10 Solid wood keel,
6+1.14PVB+6+12A+8 tempered glass

11 Lighting lamps

12 200 mm skylight/stainless-steel lamp tube

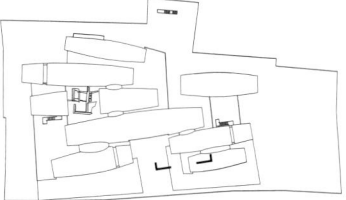

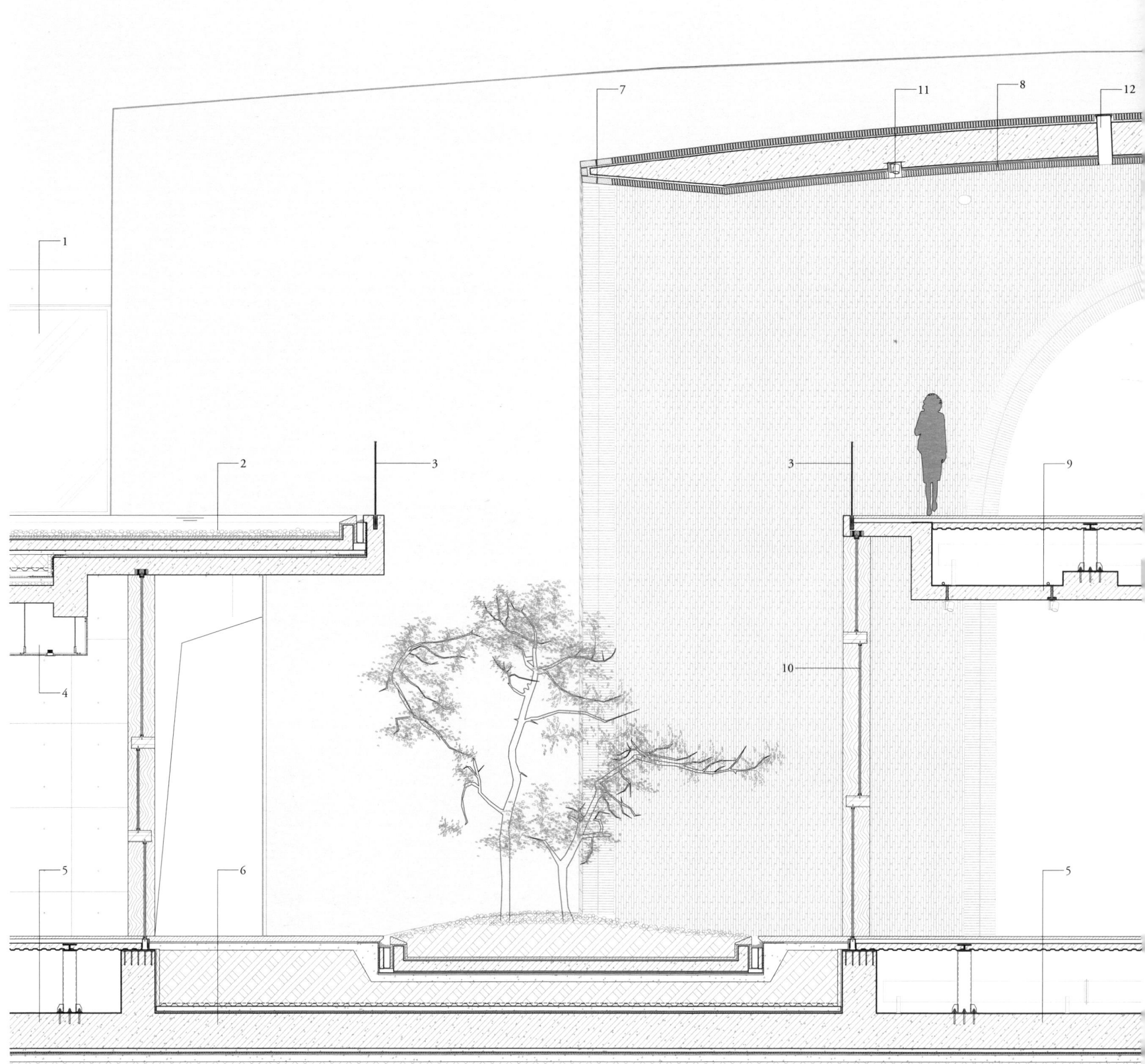

Detail B: vertical section (opposite page)

1   Kiln brick horizontal masonry; specification: 230×30×60 mm
      30 mm 1:2 cement mortar
      One 1.5 mm waterproof mortar, cement-based penetrating crystalline
      P6 impermeable reinforced-concrete structure, ends thinning
      30 mm 1:2 cement mortar
      Kiln brick horizontal masonry; specification: 230×30×60 mm

2   New and reclaimed kiln brick masonry; specification: 230×30×60 mm
      30 mm 1:2 cement mortar
      One 1.5 mm waterproof mortar, cement-based penetrating crystalline
      P6 impermeable reinforced-concrete vault structure
      60 mm dry, hard insulation rock wool board
      30 mm 1:2 cement mortar
      Kiln brick masonry; specification: 230×30×60 mm

3   8 mm consolidated wooden floor
      5 mm foam padding
      15 mm pine wool bottom plate, 45° diagonal laying
      20 mm 1:2.5 cement mortar leveling
      50 mm LC7.5 lightweight aggregate concrete
      Reinforced-concrete floor

4   80 mm granite floor
      30 mm 1:3 dry, hard cement mortar bonding layer
      100 mm Cl5 plain concrete cushion
      Plain soil compaction

5   40 mm granite floor
      60 mm 1:3 dry, hard cement mortar bonding layer
      Steel corrugated sheet and 100 mm concrete pouring
      Equipment interlayer
      10 mm 1:2 cement mortar protective layer
      One 1.5 mm waterproof mortar, cement-based penetrating crystalline
      P6 impermeable reinforced-concrete floor

6   6+1.52PVB+6 tempered laminated glass panel

7   Solid wood keel
      6+1.14PVB+6+12A+8 tempered glass

8   80 mm granite floor
      30 mm 1:3 dry, hard cement mortar bonding layer
      100 mm Cl5 plain concrete cushion
      Plain soil compaction
      200 g/m^3 non-woven filter layer
      Concave-convex drainage board
      70 mm C20 fine stone concrete protective layer
      0.4 mm polyethylene plastic film isolation layer
      4+3 mm SBS-modified bituminous waterproofing membrane
      20 mm cement mortar leveling layer
      (The thinnest part is) 40 mm aerated fragmented concrete
      topping forming slop
      P6 impermeable concrete roof

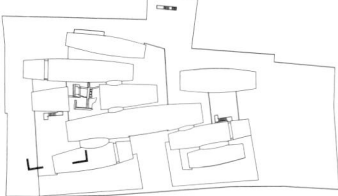

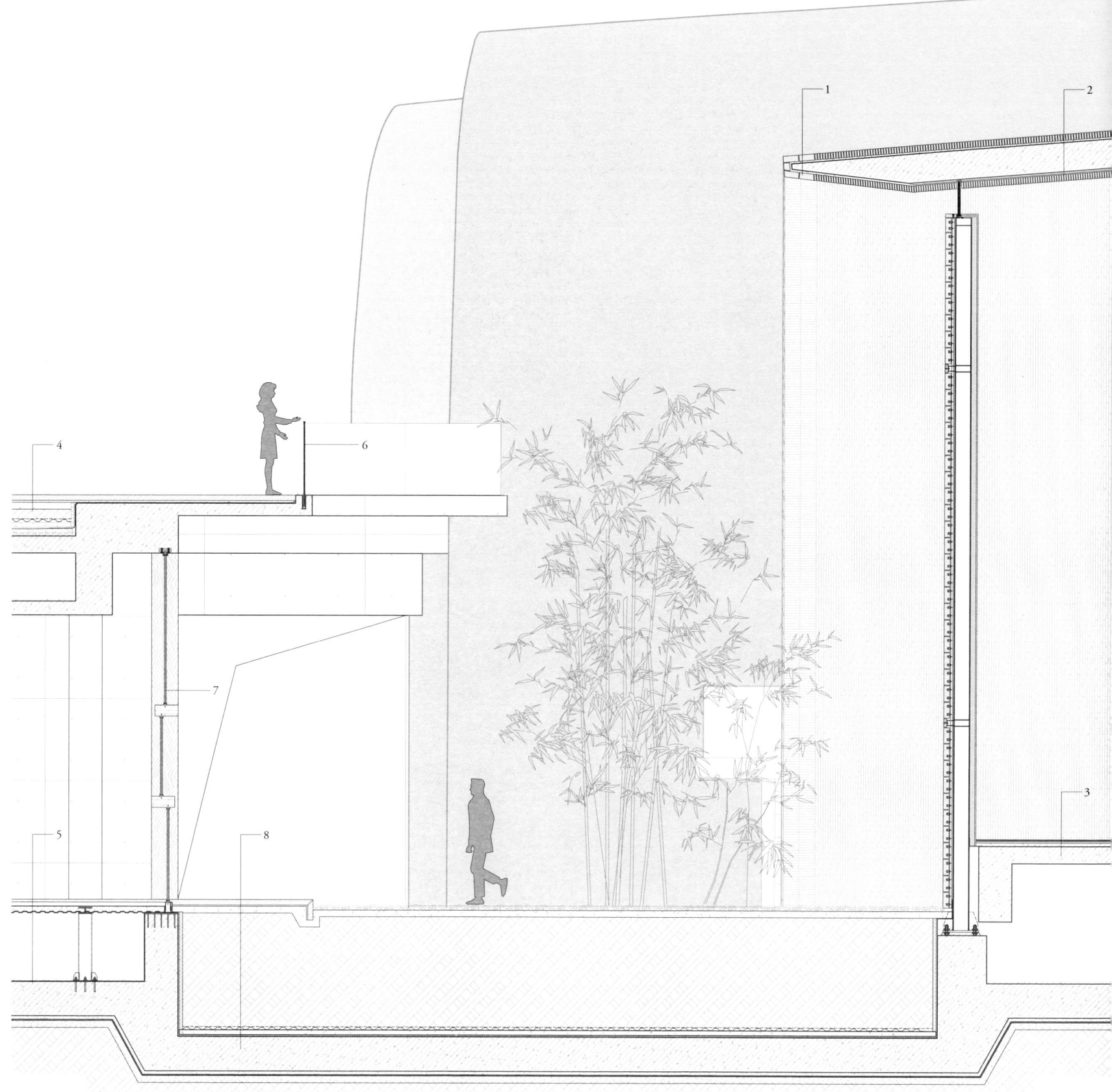

Detail C: vertical section (opposite page)

1. 300 mm fair-faced concrete beam
   40 mm stainless-steel canopy
   40 mm stainless-steel door frame
   8+1.52PVB+8 laminated extra clear tempered glass

2. 80 mm granite floor
   30 mm 1: 3 dry, hard cement mortar bonding layer
   100 mm screed
   Plain soil compaction
   50 mm fine aggregate concrete
   Polyethylene film
   4+3 mm SBS-modified bituminous waterproofing membrane
   20 mm 1:2.5 mortar layer
   P6 impermeable reinforced-concrete floor with fair-faced concrete bottom

3. 200 mm high fair-faced concrete beam
   Solid wood ventilation shutters

4. White waterproof latex paint sprayed on the top
   Aluminum alloy tuyere
   600×300 mm white tiles

5. 90×40 mm aluminum C-profile framing suspended by tie rods
   12 mm flame-retardant panel
   2 mm moisture-resistant gypsum board
   White oak veneer

6. Fair-faced concrete wall

7. Kiln brick horizontal masonry; specification: 230×30×60 mm
   30 mm 1:2 cement mortar
   One 1.5 mm waterproof mortar, cement-based penetrating crystalline
   P6 impermeable reinforced-concrete structure, ends thinning
   30 mm 1:2 cement mortar
   Kiln brick horizontal masonry; specification: 230×30×60 mm

8. Water
   50 mm black pebble, grain size 50–70 mm
   600×600×30 mm gray granite
   20 mm 1:3 cement mortar binding layer
   150 mm reinforced-concrete pool
   20 mm 1:3 mortar protective layer
   2 mm PVC waterproofing membrane
   20 mm 1:3 mortar layer
   100 mm plain concrete cushion
   Plain soil compaction

9. 40 mm granite floor
   60 mm 1:3 dry, hard cement mortar bonding layer
   100 mm plain concrete cushion
   Plain soil compaction
   P6 impermeable reinforced-concrete floor

10. Solid wood keel
    6+1.14PVB+6+12A+8 tempered glass

11. Equipment pipeline well
    5 mm 1:2 mortar protective layer
    1.5 mm cement-based infiltration crystallization
    10 mm 1:2 mortar layer
    240 mm kiln brick masonry, plain brick wall

12. Reinforced-concrete wall with fair-faced concrete inner surface
    1.5 mm cement-based infiltration crystallization
    10 mm 1:2 mortar protective layer

13. New and reclaimed kiln brick masonry; specification: 230×30×60 mm
    30 mm 1:2 mortar layer
    1.5 mm cement-based infiltration crystallization
    P6 impervious reinforced-concrete structure
    60 mm dry, hard insulation rock wool board
    30 mm 1:2 mortar layer
    Kiln brick masonry; specification: 230×30×60 mm

14. 40 mm granite floor
    60 mm 1:3 dry, hard cement mortar bonding layer
    40 mm steel corrugated sheet with 100 mm concrete pouring
    Equipment interlayer
    10 mm 1:2 mortar protective layer
    1.5 mm cement-based infiltration crystallization
    Reinforced-concrete floor with fair-faced concrete bottom

15. 40 mm granite floor
    60 mm 1:3 dry, hard cement mortar bonding layer
    Steel corrugated sheet with 100 mm concrete pouring
    Equipment interlayer
    10 mm 1:2 mortar protective layer
    1.5 mm cement-based infiltration crystallization
    P6 impermeable reinforced-concrete floor slab

16. Lighting lamps

17. 200 mm skylight/stainless-steel lamp tube

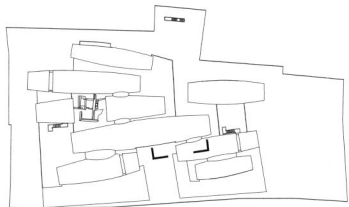

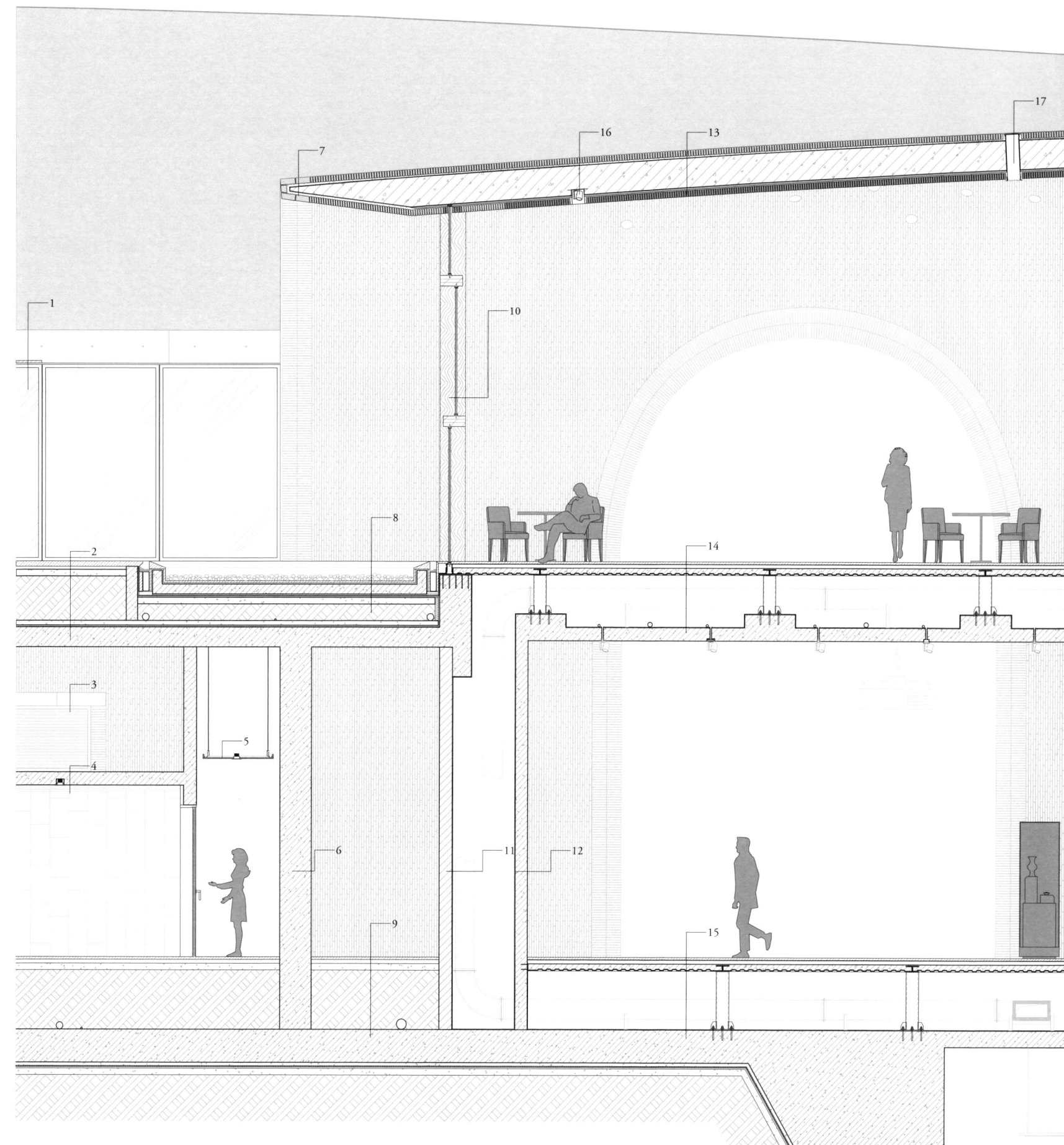

Realization

Foundation	2016
Structure	2017–2018
Mechanical equipment installation	2018
Curtain wall	2018–2019
Exhibition installation	2020

The exhibition halls of the museum are mainly located on the ground level and underground level, with the foyer located on the ground level. This arrangement allows visitors to approach the building with a sense of affinity and be impressed by its scale, which is close to that of existing buildings in the city; more importantly, the spatial experience that visitors entering the building encounter is very similar to that experienced by the craftspeople who entered brick kilns in the past.

As they meander through the Imperial Kiln Factory Heritage Park, moving between scattered bamboo groves and pebbled sections, crunching gravel under their shoes, they will view in the distance a group of long, gently lying, low brick vaults resting serenely beside the hills and surrounded by historical houses, factories, and residential buildings on three sides. The long pond between the Imperial Kiln ruins and the Imperial Kiln Museum gently guides the circulation. Groups of flattened lake stones lie docile under the water, sometimes peeking out, like schools of fish swimming in the water, their backs occasionally breaking the cover of the water surface. While strolling, visitors are treated to the sound of the flowing water in the pool, accompanied by the rustling of the bamboo leaves in the breeze and the chirping of birds in the trees; as if they are in a familiar bamboo forest, surrounded by streams and hills—a typical natural landscape in Jingdezhen.

Crossing the calm water via the bridge, one enters the long, vaulted foyer, which is almost shuttle-like in shape—wide and high in the middle, and gradually tightening at the sides—with wood-framed glass windows and doors at the ends. The bricks are arranged vertically to create double-curved surfaces, and the top of the vaults is pierced with numerous small circular skylights, like the wood throwing/observational holes in a traditional brick kiln.

From the foyer, moving right, through the bookstore and café, visitors finally arrive at the tearoom which is the semi-exterior space of the vault structure; the shimmering waters of the pond under the sunlight reflect wavy ripples on the rough surface of the brick that glide across in iridescent stripes. The low, horizontal opening here curiously suggests that visitors sit on the ground; on doing so, they receive an unexpected surprise: the long, horizontal ground surface of the Imperial Kiln Museum archaeological site is led into view when one is eye-level with the opening. This is different from the spatial experience of viewing the Longzhu Pavilion in the Imperial Kiln ruins through the vertical slits in the wall prior to entering the hallway, yet the feeling of surprise is similar.

From the foyer, moving left, at the end of the double-height exhibition hall, they can either look down at the underground galleries, rest their eyes on the sunken courtyard planted with bamboo and enclosed by the restoration studio behind the transparent glass wall, or even take in the view of the urban residential buildings that form the backdrop of the museum. To the left of the end, visitors can cross the vault to the vestibule of the auditorium shaped by brick vaults and fair-faced concrete walls; to the right of the end, huge vaults "cracked" by occasional slits of natural light invite them to cross through to the semi-outdoor vaulted space, where the archaeological site—located 6.6 feet (2 meters) below ground level—is sandwiched between two open vaults at the north and south, with the outdoor amphitheater under the northern vault and the semi-outdoor exhibition hall under the southern one.From here, visitors can look over to the archaeological site and the sunken courtyard and cityscape in the distance, or descend to the site and rest on the steps of the amphitheater to soak-in the ambiance. They are then led to another relatively smaller vaulted indoor gallery for a walk-through, where the "route" ends with a very gentle fair-faced concrete staircase, which takes them down to the underground space. Five sunken bamboo courtyards of varying sizes and shapes are scattered along the main circulation at the end of each gallery, not only allowing a modicum of natural light and ventilation within the underground space, but more importantly, they also present the opportunity for visitors to step into a courtyard at any time, as they walk into different rooms, to take breaks, pause, and even observe museum staff restore historical porcelain in the restoration room. Eventually, visitors are led to the stairs in the gap between the two vaults, where they can reach out and touch old kiln bricks burnished with kiln sweat, to be then guided by the natural light filtering in back to the starting point, with the foyer on the left and the auditorium on the right.

The auditorium is under a standalone vault with a high dome, and has relatively steep seating and a podium at the end. When Arata Isozaki visited the Imperial Kiln Museum, he called it a "spiritual space" akin to a church; it is no longer a black box that shuts out all distractions on the outside. A narrow horizontal slit has been cut along the western side of the vault and flushed with the water surface so visitors in the vault can view a reflection of the Imperial Kiln Factory site (that sits on the western side) captured against a background of lake stones in the water. A narrow vertical slit has been cut into the end of the north side wall, capturing the sky, the urban landscape, and the sunken courtyard. As a result, people can feel the slightest change in the elements outside, at any time, even though they are sitting in the auditorium.

The permanent circulation is completed by a closed horizontal up-and-down loop. The temporary circulation can be incorporated into this loop and integrated into the overall circulation, or serve as a separate circulation, as it has its own separate entrance and exit. Another feature of the museum is the integration of the porcelain restoration process as an important part of the exhibits. The office entrance is located at the north end of a relatively separate vault at the southeastern part of the building group, as it is tranquil and secluded here. Lorries can back into the vault at a loading area from the south end, which is enclosed and safe for loading and unloading.

In a word, at the Imperial Kiln Museum, visitors walk through a series of gray spaces shaped by architecture and nature. The vault structure, together with five sunken courtyards, creates a porous architecture with void and solid interlocked, and interior and exterior intertwined. Inside the museum, visitors will find themselves captured by a feeling that is both familiar and alien. The rich lighting effects presented by the natural light that is guided in leads them to meander around the space, piquing their curiosity to explore, moving them from one space to another. This eventually creates a museum journey that reconciles the kiln, the porcelain, and the people.

The concept of the Jingdezhen Imperial Kiln Museum originated from the perception of Jingdezhen's unique regional culture and the local people's wisdom for surviving. It subverts our traditional cognition of museums, constructs a porous and open space system, blends with the surrounding nature and cultural environment, and creates an innovative and contemporary museum experience. Despite facing a global architectural practice dominated by technological ecological concepts, the Jingdezhen Imperial Kiln Museum has achieved the profound practice of "Architecture of Nature" with its own intelligent nature and ecological notions.

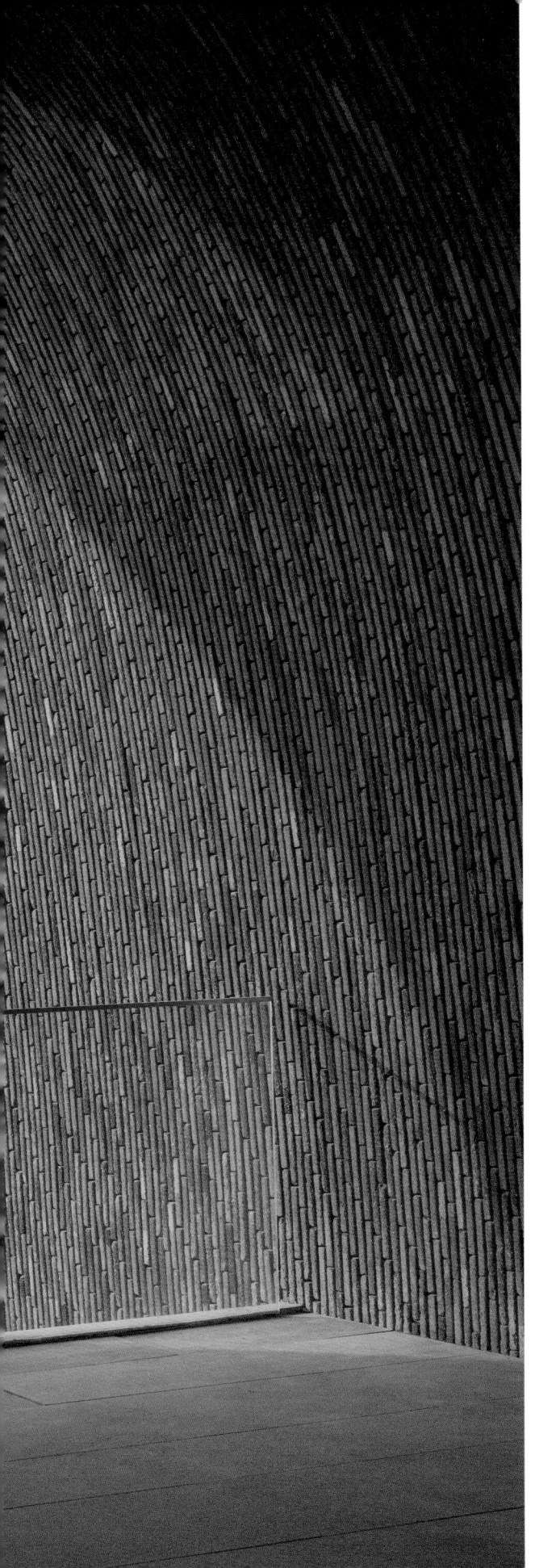

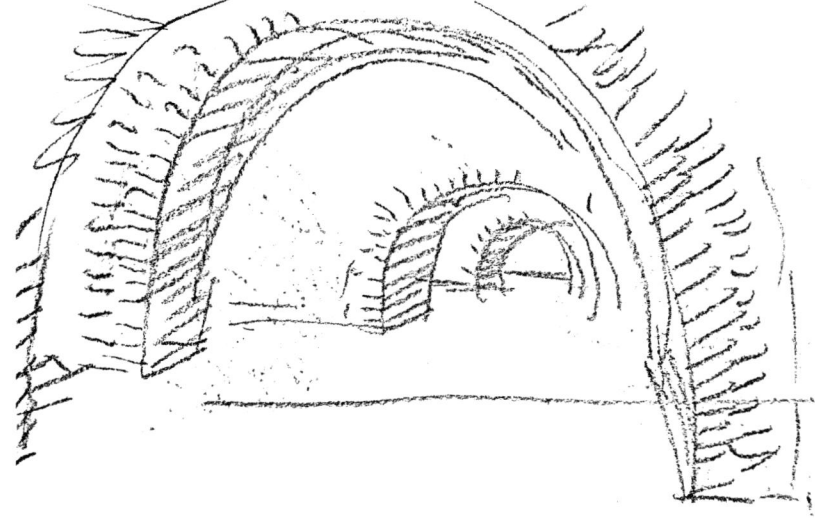

Opening Exhibition

September 19–October 10, 2020
Jingdezhen Imperial Kiln Museum

Transformation—A Joint Exhibition of the Four Contemporary
Masters from CAFA and the Opening Exhibition of Jingdezhen
Imperial Kiln Museum

Fan Di'an

President, Central Academy of Fine Arts

Chairman, China Artists Association

In the time of mid-autumn, in the year of *Gengzi*—the Chinese equivalent of year 2020—Jingdezhen Imperial Kiln Museum, designed by Zhu Pei, was completed and opened to the public, which not only adds a brand-new cultural landmark to Jingdezhen—the Millennium Capital of Porcelain—but the museum also presents itself as a masterpiece in contemporary architecture with unique Chinese cultural characteristics that are also full of contemporary creative wisdom.

Zhu Pei, a famous contemporary architect, took on this project with much enthusiasm, studying in depth Jingdezhen's traditional cultural heritage, to devote himself to a cultural and ideological construction. When it came to the design of the museum, he took the Imperial Kiln sites as the starting point and extracted the basic idea of vaults from ancient kilns, so as to make the museum unique and natural, both in function and culture. As one takes a stroll outside and looks at its shape from a distance, one can admire the museum as a monument of ceramic culture; wandering among the complex and looking inside, into its essence, one can touch the traces of the olden craftspeoples' ingenuity, which has been impressive and spectacular across time and space throughout Jingdezhen's history.

Today, the glory of the times rises out of a millennium "kiln fire." In the museum's opening exhibition entitled "Transformation," the works of Xu Bing, Sui Jianguo, Liu Xiaodong, and Zhu Pei—four contemporary artists from CAFA (Central Academy of Fine Arts) with extensive international influence—were jointly exhibited. These works condensed and reflected the evolution and renewal of Chinese contemporary art ideas and methodologies since the start of the new century. Having gone through formal academic education and been deeply immersed in cultural heritage, the four artists are bold to have leapt out of the box, stepping off the beaten path to allow themselves to be fired by the magnificent flames of the tremendous changes of the era brought about by globalization. They continued moving forward and have reproduced the changes of society through their personal concepts and innovative language, which are to be celebrated with worldwide honor. "Transformation," in their artistic experience, not only directly refers to history and reality, and creation and humanities, but also represents the inheritance and sublimation of their artistic creation.

The contemporary development of Jingdezhen City has also experienced transformation, like the ceramics in a kiln fire. By protecting the ceramic industrial heritage, the city creates a cultural and industrial ecology of ceramics. Through introducing top art, the city's taste in culture is improved. The exchanges and cooperation between CAFA and Jingdezhen are based on the common vision of revitalizing the ceramics industry and strengthening the confidence of Chinese culture. It is expected that in the future, Jingdezhen will transform from the ceramics export hub of the ancient Silk Road to an art city of the Silk Road Economic Belt and the 21st-Century Maritime Silk Road, bringing together more artists, architects, and thinkers, adding fuel to the cultural furnace to make the "transformed" city shine with the glory of a new era.

Wang Mingxian

Scholar of Architecture and Art History, Chinese National Academy of Arts
Visiting Professor, School of Architecture, Central Academy of Fine Arts

Since the 1990s, the trend toward Chinese Experimental Architecture has been rising, with the emergence of a number of internationally recognized experimental buildings that have changed the faces of contemporary Chinese architecture history. The Imperial Kiln Museum, designed by Zhu Pei, is a masterpiece of contemporary Chinese architecture and a landmark work among Chinese Experimental Architecture. The architect has delved into the cultural and climatic roots of Jingdezhen, revealed the consanguinity of its people, the kilns, and porcelain, and redefined the concept of space and time in the museum. The Imperial Kiln Museum pays homage to Jingdezhen City, the "Millennium Capital of Art" of Chinese porcelain, and also serves as an expression of high regard to China's future cities and architectural art by delicately implanting new concepts from modern reflections.

Astute scholars would have noticed a cultural turn taking place in the current field of international architecture, and Zhu Pei's theory of "Architecture of Nature" is, accordingly, a response to it. The Imperial Kiln Museum is a tectonic experiment on the theory of "Architecture of Nature". Based on thoughts on the contemporaneity of the oriental view of nature, Zhu Pei has constructed a type of intelligent, cultural and ecological "Architecture of Nature", and explored the profound relationship among humanity, nature and culture, which together form a genre of its own, lead a trend for contemporary architecture, and display an extremely important research significance and value.

Arata Isozaki

Architect

Laureate, Pritzker Architecture Prize

Let's take the opportunity to rediscover the Jingdezhen culture.

Porcelain—its history and tradition; design and function; pursuit of geometry and technology; rarity and rationality of production; the workshops for the perception of soil and flame; and visitors that come from afar to experience it—all these constitute the local culture polished by the hands of people living in Jingdezhen throughout the years. The land where they dwelled is known as the Millennium Capital of Porcelain.

With reputation comes great difficulties for architects during construction. But don't worry, because here, the architecture—however designed—will always bear the unique traits of the porcelain of the city.

As the cultural symbol of the Millennium Capital of Porcelain, the Imperial Kiln Museum has been meticulously designed, in terms of creating a cultural space to reflect the pursuit of balance.

Whatever the construction project is, it should take into account the economic, urban, and social impacts; but the historical context at the site cannot be deciphered merely with the visible streetscape. The motivation to reinterpret the long history buried deep underground and connect it with modern urban public functions actually forms the constituent elements of the museum.

If you actually visit the Imperial Kiln Museum, you can delve into the magnificent royal stories behind it and enjoy a great sense of serenity in the space. Moreover, you will also perceive a sense of fluidity created by the breeze while admiring the beauty of natural light interwoven with shadow.

This is an epoch-making opening exhibition. Only such an architecture can expand the boundary of the connotation of "porcelain," gradually breaking the barriers of time and space, and unleashing the vitality and emotions of contemporary artists.

This is the answer given by Zhu Pei's work, which stands here today on the soil of the city as a masterpiece of contemporary Jingdezhen.

On the occasion of the opening of Jingdezhen Imperial Kiln Museum, please allow me to extend my heartfelt wishes.

Rem Koolhaas

Architect

Laureate, Pritzker Architecture Prize

I'm very happy to participate in the opening of the Imperial Kiln Museum by Zhu Pei. I haven't seen the building yet, but I've really studied it; I've listened to explanations about it, and I think it's an extremely significant, very subtle building that introduces a number of very promising things in China in a very impressive way. I think it establishes a very intelligent context. It has a very smart relationship with the existing context, but it does something completely new and unexpected with that, in a sense, not only through one kind of history, but a number of histories that come together at this place. So, I think there is—although it is very sensitive—nothing conservative about it. On the contrary, I think it's a really new way of treating architecture as an element that can connect and make relation, and establish relationships between very different elements.

Steven Holl

Principal, Steven Holl Architects

Tenured Professor of Architecture, Graduate School of Architecture, Planning and Preservation,
Columbia University

I want to make a few remarks on Zhu Pei's Imperial Kiln Museum. Being here in New York, I thought to myself, "What is architecture excellence today?" It should do five things: It should positively express our time; it should remain engaged with the local side of history; it should employ natural light and ventilation, and be of ecological excellence; it should have spatial energy; and it should have a poetic material expression. And Zhu Pei's architecture, the Imperial Kiln Museum in Jingdezhen, does all of these things, and does it with excellence. That's really rare. In fact, I think it's a masterpiece of an architecture.

Thomas Krens

Curator

Former Director, Solomon R. Guggenheim Foundation

On the occasion of the opening of the Jingdezhen Imperial Kiln Museum, I would like to offer my sincere congratulations to Zhu Pei, the architect of this extraordinary new building in one of China's great cities. I first started working with Zhu Pei more than fifteen years ago, on a series of cultural projects in China; prior to our current project, perhaps our most significant joint venture was to produce a cultural master plan for Tai Miao, the imperial ancestral shrine attached to the Forbidden City in Beijing. The current design for our new project evolves directly from Tai Miao, and I am particularly struck by its visual similarities in the Jingdezhen Imperial Kiln Museum. All great architects have a subtle signature, a distinct form of three-dimensional calligraphy; Zhu Pei's new museum for Jingdezhen is but the latest impressive creative statement from one of China's great creative artists. I would like to offer my sincere expression of admiration on this new building, to Zhu Pei, and to the citizens of Jingdezhen.

Xu Bing
Background Story: Endless Brooks and Mountains, 2014
Multimedia installation
70.9×425.2 in (180×1,080 cm)

Xu Bing
*Square Word Calligraphy: "Preface to The Poems
Composed at The Orchid Pavilion" by Wang Xizhi*, 2017
Ink on paper
75×358 in (191×909 cm)

Sui Jianguo

1   *Cloud Garden-Planting Trace2# Prototype*, 2017
Sensitive resin
15.6×9.8×7.9 in (39.5×25×20 cm)

2   *Cloud Garden-Planting Trace2#*, 2018
Sensitive resin, steel frame
472.4×236.2×236.2 in (1,200×600×600 cm)

Liu Xiaodong
Dong, 2005
Hometown Boy, 2010
Uummannaq Children's Home, 2017
Digital video series

Liu Xiaodong
Diary of an Empty City 2, 2015
Oil on canvas
98.4×118.1 in (250×300 cm)

(following pages) Zhu Pei
Models of the design process of the Imperial Kiln Museum, 2016–2020
Various materials
Variable sizes

Zhu Pei
Art installation of Kiln Bricks Masonry, 2020
Kiln brick, curtain, light box
70.9×661.4×47.2 in (180×1,680×120 cm)

Zhu Pei
Sketches of the Imperial Kiln Museum, 2020
Curtain, light box
33.5×850.4×189 in (85×2,160×480 cm)

石材

内部为毛石墙砌
找与砖之间

A Symbol of the City that Condenses on the Earth

—A Conversation about Work with Zhu Pei

Fang Lili

Jingdezhen Imperial Kiln Museum
September 21, 2020

Introduction

In mid to late September 2020, the Jingdezhen Imperial Kiln Museum, designed by Professor Zhu Pei, held its opening exhibition titled "Transformation—A Joint Exhibition of the Four Contemporary Masters from CAFA" after its completion. At that time, I happened to be in Jingdezhen leading a team of graduate students on a field study, and so, to extend the educational value of the trip, I visited the exhibition with my students.

Having studied Jingdezhen for many years, I know the importance of the Imperial Kiln Factory (the site of Imperial Kilns), and know that it is definitely a landmark in the city. Building a museum here is to build a cultural symbol for the city, which is something extraordinary, for Jingdezhen's reputation through history as well as the "legitimacy" of the term "Jingdezhen" itself both extend from this factory that was built by emperors of past eras.

Jingdezhen Imperial Kiln Factory was the site of royal kilns during the Ming and Qing dynasties. Being a sacred porcelain-making place for the emperors, much reverence was given to the site and it was selected with much respect and attention. From the top of a hill at the center of Jingdezhen, one can get a splendid panoramic view of the city. During the Tang dynasty, people believed that the hill was surrounded by five dragons, hence it was named Pearl Hill, originating from the well-known saying "five dragons grabbing a pearl." At the beginning of the Ming dynasty, the Imperial Court regarded the beneficial topography of Pearl Hill very highly and set up a royal wares factory there, which was changed to the royal kiln factory in the Qing dynasty. During that reign, Pearl Hill came to be referred to as *zhen* hill, to mean a mountain that can seal and dispel evil spirits.

The surrounding walls of the Imperial Kiln Factory, according to the book *Pottery Records of Jingdezhen*, spanned the hill and stretched for about three *li* (Chinese miles), which was about 4,921 feet (1,500 meters). The buildings were constructed in typical feudal government-run factory style, and were built according to certain rules and specifications.

Humans have long been creatures that believe in divinity, and it is the implantation of this divinity in one's mind that separates humans from animals. That is why, when humans built places of dwelling in ancient times, they always included a place for God, and that is why traditional buildings are often spaces of living for both human beings and God. Just like how the legitimacy of traditional European cities used to lie in the church, in China, the legitimacy of villages used to lie in their ancestral temples where people worshiped ancestors. With regard to the Imperial Kiln Factory in Jingdezhen, the buildings' legitimacy lay not only in the sacredness of the selected site, but also in the presence of God—three temples had been built within the surrounding walls of the factory: Imperial Pottery God Temple, Guandi Temple, and Earth God Temple.

According to the perspectives of anthropology, to form a pattern for human behaviors, there should be a set of symbolic traditions to establish this pattern. Those traditions consist of a series of symbols that are not only the expression, media, and relevance of our biological, psychological, and social existence, but which are also the preconditions for these three types of existence. Meaning, people's individual behavior is guided not only by a set of value systems, but also by a symbol that embodies the value system—that is, people's behaviors are effectively motivated not by their physical/body movements; instead, they follow a certain culture or tradition, which is defined by a series of symbols. All living things on earth are subject to their own natural laws. Only humans are free to build their living space into whatever form they wish it to be. However, this freedom is also restricted by the symbolic representation of the world in which one lives. Human beings are the only "animal" to understand the world by symbols. Without symbols, intuition alone can hardly help us understand the world. In traditional society, the architecture where humans and God coexisted was an important symbol, as well as a carrier of the culture of the times.

However, after the Industrial Revolution, the idea that God was no longer with people became the more sought after and accepted notion. The construction of new cities no longer focused on describing the understanding of "Heaven, Earth, Space, and God," but focused instead on the feelings of humans themselves. It was the same in Jingdezhen. Therefore, in the time between the Republic of China period to earlier recent times, the Imperial Kiln Factory and the three temples on the site were demolished. The place later became the seat of the government of Fuliang County and Jingdezhen Municipality, successively.

During the industrial era, technologies helped humans surmount the limitations of natural resources and climate formation in different regions, and buildings all over the world became infinitely similar. Countless cities began to lose their particularity and legitimacy. Legitimacy, in essence, translates to cultural value. Without particularities, the cultural value of a city will be questioned.

These days, as diversity in cultures is increasingly valued, many cities have begun to look for their new legitimacy. And how a city can construct this new legitimacy is definitely an idea that is worthy of deep thought. After visiting Professor Zhu Pei's Imperial Kiln Museum, I realized immediately that the new legitimacy of a city lies in the restructuring and reconstruction of its history. The accumulation of history will become the cultural resources and symbols of new buildings, based on which human beings are shaping the new urban landscape.

But presenting history does not mean displaying its original state, rather, its about a poetic reinterpretation through re-understanding. Sometime after divinity was gone, humans started searching for the existence of spirituality, which was offered through the echoes of history in people's minds, and through human beings' link with the local natural environment. Perhaps, this was when humankind began to temper divinity worship with cravings for spirituality, and to explore new legitimacies for cities. In Professor Zhu Pei's design of the Imperial Kiln Museum, I heard the echoes of the ancient footsteps of Jingdezhen's pottery craftspeople in the street; felt the cool air coming through the traditional *lilongs* (narrow lanes between houses); appreciated the murmur of the brooks in traditional villages producing raw materials for the porcelain; and immersed in the vibe of ancient Jingdezhen as a "Town of Year-round Thunder and Lightning." All these elements constitute the spirituality of Jingdezhen.

The museum building represents the city's pursuit for a new legitimacy and a new cultural trait. It is an architecture with symbolic meanings. Therefore, it is no longer just a building, but a city symbol condensed on the earth. Its existence is to tell the history and stories of the city to all who come here, and also to project the value system embodied in the architecture onto the city's residents, forming a part of their behavior patterns. If we understand the building from this perspective, it has a very profound meaning. I have been working on a collection of writings that discuss a hundred years of changes in Jingdezhen and came to realize that the building of the Imperial Kiln Museum is a major event in the history of Jingdezhen, and that I need to properly understand this building in order to accurately describe its significance and value.

To this end, I had two conversations with Professor Zhu Pei, one in a café and the second at the site of the museum, where I followed him with my students to observe every detail of the building. I believe these two conversations I had with Professor Zhu Pei are very important. They are the communication between an architect and an anthropologist. During the talks, I gained a deeper understanding of his concept and conception of designing the museum, and I began to realize that the building would become a milestone in oriental architectural philosophy, and would become a new discourse space that promotes the diversity of contemporary architecture, in which human beings would rebuild the spirituality and legitimacy of the city.

In short, humankind is standing at the entrance of a new era, embracing a leap forward, both in science and technology, as well as embracing humanistic concepts in which high technology and high human needs coexist. I hope that the Imperial Kiln Museum designed by Professor Zhu Pei will become a carrier, representing not only the Jingdezhen of today, but also the Jingdezhen of the future, as well as be an important cultural symbol throughout the history of Jingdezhen.

The following is a script of my talks with Professor Zhu Pei. I hope readers will gather positive take-aways from it that benefit them.

Architecture of Nature, Smart Architecture

Fang Lili: Professor Zhu, it's a pleasure to meet you. Today, I visited the Jingdezhen Imperial Kiln Museum. It's very impressive. I noticed that in the introduction part of the exhibition, you underscored that your architecture is an "Architecture of Nature," that is to say, it grows from nature. I am quite fascinated by this concept. I think architecture should first deal with the relationship between human beings and nature, both defending and harnessing nature. It is the medium and bridge connecting human and nature. What's your idea on this?

Zhu Pei: I have always been interested in the relationship between architecture, people, and nature. I think that if we humans could make good use of nature, our buildings will be very smart. For example, we don't build buildings meant for a cold zone in a tropical rainforest; all buildings are built to adapt to nature. But in the modern world, we use technologies to copy-paste and build the same type of buildings everywhere in the world. There are two subtexts: one is the waste of energy, because energy is needed to promote the existence of modern buildings, such as heating in cold climates and air conditioning in hot climates; otherwise, people cannot survive or live comfortably. The other is that modern buildings represent a stupid—that is, an unwise—behavior, which means that they cannot adapt to the local environment or utilize natural resources well, resulting in not only the waste of energy, but also the destruction of nature. So, in essence, we're creating technologies, while destroying ourselves with them. Because of this, I began to deeply explore Chinese natural philosophy and re-explore the relationship between architecture and nature, as well as between architecture and humans. I think Chinese natural philosophy is not traditional, but, in fact, very contemporary, because the world needs a wisdom which adapts to nature, instead of one created by technologies. In fact, the communication between man and nature has wisdom in itself. As long as we can understand nature, we will master the wisdom of architecture, and this wisdom will materialize.

Fang Lili: I'm impressed by the concept of smart architecture. Such buildings are suited for both human dwelling and the buildings' local climatic conditions, and they can also make effective use of local natural resources. Such buildings adapt to the specific environment and climate, as if they have been grown naturally in the local soil, therefore, they are brimming with wisdom inspired by nature. But with the advent of technology, man no longer continued to care about the relationship between architecture and climate, between architecture and local materials, or even between architecture and specific species. When these relationships were discarded, they began to replace everything with technology, together with creations that resulted from technology. As a result, modern architecture dominated the world, cutting off its relationship with climate conditions, natural resources, and the cultural practices developed specific to each environment.

All urban buildings have become increasingly homogeneous. Technologies have created so many "foreign objects" on the earth, which will eventually turn into garbage that cannot be recycled, only bringing damage to the environment. All fauna and flora are symbiotic with the rhythm of the earth, except humans, who use technology to produce a lot of things unfriendly to nature and the earth. These things cannot adapt to the earth, nor grow within the networks of nature. They do not resonate with nature. They come from outside nature and are not ecological or smart. In the past, we believed that science and technology would build a more orderly world for humankind, however, the law of entropy says that technology is only an energy converter, which increases the input power of the product and accelerates the process of entropy. As a result, the higher the degree of modernization of the world, the higher the entropy, and thus, the greater the likelihood of turmoil.

Therefore, my understanding is that good architecture is smart because it grows from nature, which is consistent with the local natural environment, culture, and history. It is a way of low entropy, as well as environmental protection, isn't it?

Zhu Pei: Yes, "Architecture of Nature" refers to architecture that is intelligent, energy-efficient, and which can also highlight local culture. Therefore, in general, "Architecture of Nature" has its roots in climate and culture. For example, if the Imperial Kiln Museum had been designed in a conventional way, the entrance would have been made into a magnificent tall glass atrium and the exhibition hall would have been made into a big black box because a typical museum usually does not use natural light, but electrical light. However, today's Jingdezhen Imperial Kiln Museum completely breaks away from the concept of traditional museums to be an unconventional contemporary building designed on a concept that uses Jingdezhen's traditional kiln as a prototype. It is arranged along the north–south direction with two ends open, allowing natural wind to flow in and sunlight to come through, and it is low-rise, modest, and space-efficient.

Soulful Architecture, Landscape Architecture

Fang Lili: I have long been hearing about the museum. Many people were looking forward to it, even before it was finished. Despite the museum's preceding reputation and all the prior discussions and imaginations I had about it, I still feel very excited when viewing it in person. It is an enriching visual and mental experience, almost like a déjà vu, as if it has always been here, simply waiting for us to discover its presence, seemingly telling us that it grows from here and that this is where it has belonged all along. It is bold and ingenious to design the Imperial Kiln Museum into a kiln for making porcelain, which also touches the soul of the city. I dare to say this because I have spent more than two decades doing research in Jingdezhen and have a deep understanding of the city. The kiln is the most important aspect of all the production processes, because if the fire in the kiln does not burn well, all the previous work—no matter how well-made—would be wasted. It is said that farmers depend on the weather for their food, while pottery craftspeople rely on fire for their bread; that is why the porcelain industry is sometimes called the kiln industry. I wonder how did you get this inspiration?

Zhu Pei: In order to complete this idea, I walked around the traditional *lilongs* (narrow lanes between houses) in Jingdezhen over and over again. Just like how you anthropologists conduct field research, I, too, needed to observe and think while being out in the field. "Why are the old buildings in Jingdezhen like this; and why are there so many kiln houses and workshops among the *lilongs*?" I thought about the behavior of the city's artisans and residents, the relationship between the Chang River and the city, and between the surrounding hills and the city.

During my observation and review, I found that there were not many branches of *lilongs* in this city and there had been no planning for them in the construction process. However, everyone seemed to have enough awareness that there should be no dead ends; this was likely because of a matter of convenience and orderliness, so that goods could be shipped to Chang River by way of shortcuts. This was because there were many private kilns and workshops in the *lilongs* comprising kiln houses, workshops, and residential houses—an important feature of Jingdezhen City. These kiln and workshops were like cell nucleus, and in between, the locals built residential and commercial buildings; together, these constituted the special texture of the city. Kilns are very important for the city, they are the soul. In Jingdezhen, kilns were built along the river and the city was formed based on these kilns, so, Jingdezhen is a city that is shaped long and narrow, like a strip, stretching from north to south.

Fang Lili: Indeed. The kiln is not only the soul of Jingdezhen, but also the cultural landscape of Jingdezhen. The kilns in ancient Jingdezhen were very dense. The flames in a kiln would jet out of the chimney almost 7 to 10 feet (2 to 3 meters) high, lighting up the night sky. Ancient Jingdezhen featured a workshop-style division of labor, with greenware houses (specialized in molding) and kilns (for firing porcelain) around, as well as studios for glazing. After the greenware was made, someone would ship it to the kiln for burning, so the *lilong* cannot be too long and cannot have many turnings. Greenware-shipping was tiring, but also technical, because the clay pieces could break in the process if the person did not walk steadily, or if he collides into someone by accident at a turning. In addition, *lilongs* in Jingdezhen are all interconnected because the person can only go forward, not backward. Therefore, ancient Jingdezhen's *lilongs* were formed naturally, according to the needs of that time. In ancient times, Jingdezhen was filled with hustle and bustle. By the time all the greenware was ready to be shipped to the kilns, there would be many shippers in the street. When kilning was finished, many people would use carts to ship their porcelain to studios for glazing. There were sounds of footsteps and peddling all over the street, with high flames burning into the sky at night, hence the name "Town of Year-round Thunder and Lightning" came about in ancient times. Your observation is very detailed and accurate.

Zhu Pei: Over the past four years, I have been coming to Jingdezhen dozens of times to finish this project.

Fang Lili: That's how you've captured the soul of the city. You've designed a building complex in the form of Jingdezhen kilns. These buildings are interconnected with each other, just like Jingdezhen's *lilongs*, leaving spaces in between. There are no windows in these buildings, and the light coming through the apertures breaks the darkness, which is very mysterious and sacred. It's kind of like the light in Tadao Ando's buildings, but your use of light is more diversified and changeable, and that's what I really like about it.

Context Architecture, Sensory Architecture

Fang Lili: I think the architectural complex has a local sense of context, because not only its appearance, but also its construction method and materials come from the brick kilns of Jingdezhen. I have written about Jingdezhen civilian kilns, so I know that Jingdezhen brick kilns is a generic term for civilian kilns, referring to a kiln house as the main structure. On the first floor, there would be a door and a very large space where wood was thrown to feed the fire. The enclosing (the placing of greenware into saggers—clay boxes used to hold finer ceramics during baking—and shipping them to the internal chamber) and opening (taking out the fired potteries) were also finished on this floor. The second floor was where the kiln wood was stored and the kiln workers lived. The internal chamber lay across the kiln house, half on the first floor and half on the second floor. At the top of the internal chamber on the second floor, there was a hole to monitor the fire, into which workers would spit to judge the temperature of the fire according to the speed at which the spit "rolled" in the fire. The kilns in Jingdezhen were very firm, but because of constant firing, the internal chambers would be demolished every two or three years for reconstruction. This process is referred to as *luan yao* here. I once recorded this masonry process of kilns in my book. I think it is very special as it was a creation of local craftspeople. The internal chamber was vaulted, with no pillars, nor steel frame; it was vaulted little by little. Is this method frequently used? I rarely see such methods in use. Moreover, the kilns were built with bricks. Are there any precedents in architecture on this, or is it an original system?

Zhu Pei: In the world, every region has its own unique culture. As far as space construction goes, every region has its unique wisdom and method. For example, the earliest space of humans was built of trees and rocks. The length of wood and rocks determined the span of the space. Then, the Romans invented arches, which was a revolution in the history of space construction. In the early days, the Romans made an arch support out of earth, and laid bricks and stones on it, and then poured concrete and bound bricks and stones together, and finally removed the earth to form an arch. The cross section of the arch was like a sandwich. The construction of Jingdezhen's traditional brick kilns, however, was completely different from that of the arches of the Roman Empire. They used thin bricks and viscous mud, relying on the gravity of the bricks themselves to form complex double-curved surfaces, with strong oriental vault characteristics. Instead of using scaffolding, Jingdezhen's artisans placed the bricks using the law of gravity and built the vault through staggered placement of brick layers. The construction process of the double-curved vault (locally known as the *luan yao* process) involved artisans cutting an extremely complex double-curved surface horizontally countless times along the major axis, while ensuring that the thickness of the cutting was the same as the thickness of the kiln brick. Modern architects can generate a double-curved surface with a computer, but ancient artisans turned such a complex double-curved surface into an infinite number of single-curved surfaces with their bare hands.

Fang Lili: Have you also applied this principle?

Zhu Pei: Yes, the structure of the Imperial Kiln Museum is inspired by traditional brick kilns in Jingdezhen that use the local *luan yao* method. That is why the museum is made of bricks that are of the same size as those in a traditional brick kiln, and also laid vertically.

Fang Lili: Are there any architectural breakthroughs in your techniques and methods?

Zhu Pei: Yes, in terms of how to systematize eight double-curved vaults of different sizes and curvatures. Inspired by the *luan yao* method, I invented a scaffolding system—like a centipede with retractable legs. With the help of soft and flexible formwork, the system can "walk" along the major axis, so that we can systematically construct very complex double-curved surfaces.

What made architecture smart in the past was that it involved the easiest construction methods, saving materials and energy. However, if we continue to use traditional methods to build today's buildings without understanding or critical thinking, it may backfire and violate the basic principle of smart construction.

Fang Lili: Your idea makes sense. Are these bricks specially made?

Zhu Pei: Yes, they were made from crushed saggers mixed with clay. The size is based on the size of traditional kiln bricks.

Fang Lili: The crushed saggers are lighter and the pores are larger, so you are very careful about the selection of materials.

Zhu Pei: Yes, in a word, I think to seek inspiration from the wisdom of traditional architecture and to create something that does not exist in the world in the smartest and simplest way; it is an ideal way of working because the essence of art is creating a new experience. The museums we create today are different from those of the past, which is the very meaning of the existence of contemporary architecture. Meanwhile, however, this museum is not a foreign object. It is neither counter-cultural, anti-lifestyle, nor anti-climate. It is rooted in the local natural context and historical context. This is my concept and understanding of "Architecture of Nature." So, you will feel that the building is safe and modern, but it also seems to have a lot to do with the past. The repetition of these old bricks, the environment provided by the vaults, and the bamboo forests and water outside remind us of Jingdezhen, where porcelain has been made for generations.

Fang Lili: Impressive! When I went to visit, I saw kilns lying on the ground one after another, with two ends open, and people sitting casually inside, sort of like people enjoying the cool air in the *lilongs*. Growing up in Jingdezhen, I remember, on hot summer days with no air conditioners at home, people would put a bamboo bed in the *lilong* and enjoy the cool air passing through. The *lilongs* were well ventilated, just like it is in here. I feel that the old Jingdezhen is back.

Zhu Pei: The hot summer in Jingdezhen is unbearable, especially for a northerner like me. During construction, I often cooled myself below a vault. At that time, the glass was not sealed, so both sides were open, with cool air coming through gently. Each time I sat there, it felt immediately like each vault was a wind tunnel, creating a pleasant microclimate, just like how the traditional *lilongs* were. As it turns out, the museum doesn't need air conditioning, even in summer.

Fang Lili: I think that this is a very good idea. Jingdezhen Imperial Kiln is a place where porcelain was made for the emperors. It is attached with a historical reputation; therefore, most designers would seek to make it magnificent, but you took a different path and made it down-to-earth, carrying more of the Jingdezhen vibe. You use water to separate the museum from elsewhere, so people have to pass by the water surface to reach the museum. Is it also a reflection of the philosophy of "building kilns alongside the river, and city alongside kilns?" Is this why you put kilns and water together?

Zhu Pei: As you said, porcelain is made from metal, wood, water, fire, and earth, so I wanted to convey this feeling in my architecture. As one walks toward the museum, they are not stepping on a hard ground but a soft gravel path, which crunches under the shoes. This is accompanied by the sound of bamboo swaying on both sides of the road, which leads us to the water's edge. The water also generates sounds. Usually, to enter a village, we first have to find a river surrounding the village and its water mouth. In the past, all the old villages in Jiangxi Province had a water mouth. It was like a pavilion (rest stop) on the edge of a traditional city, sort of like the physical boundary of a village, but the water mouth will continue to push the boundary forward. The boundary of the museum seems to be here, but not exactly; the water surface and graveled ground integrate it with nature little by little. That is to say, the museum is not distinct between the inside and outside and blends the void and solid.

Fang Lili: While still far away from the museum, we already heard the sound of running water. Following the sound, our eyes slowly widened to take in the sight of the museum complex. I think this is very good. How did you get the idea to keep the water flowing to make a babbling sound, like a stream?

Zhu Pei: If you enter Jingdezhen's original environment, you can often hear the sound of streams. You don't know where the stream is, but you can hear one almost constantly. It is a very delicate feeling, often accompanied by the rustling of bamboo forests. We hear the sound of streams before we even see them, and see the bamboos before we come across any house or village. Walking in the mountains of Jingdezhen, you know that where there are bamboos, there must be households. Impressed by this feeling, I planted some bamboos inside and outside of the museum.

Fang Lili: I think it is a wonderful idea to use bamboos. The bamboo groves evoke a feeling of the regions south of the Yangtze River and also convey a scholarly sense; for literati certainly love bamboos. The building you designed gives people so many delicate feelings. If you put it into the category of art, it definitely would not only meet the audience's visual and auditory demands, but also provide them with the experience of having various historical scenes and local scenes blended together. The building itself is the symbol of Jingdezhen's culture and history, which embodies the soul of Jingdezhen's craftspeople and the charm of the city. What I like most about the museum is that unlike other buildings, which have windows at the center or in the upper part of walls, you've opened a slit alongside the floor. Looking inside across the water surface, I saw multiple pairs of walking feet instead of heads. And because I looked across the water, the view created by the reflection appeared like many people wading through the water. It's really ingenious. How did you come up with that?

Zhu Pei: Actually, I took a lot of photos, right here, of the surface of the water. When you are sitting by that area, you will see people walking as though they are wading through the water. I very much like this feeling. The stones are very much like schools of fish moving inch by inch to the water surface, sometimes exposing their backs. We see those "fishes" mostly under water, but every now and then they peek through the water surface, just a little bit, to become "alive," and you feel that the building and everything is alive.

Fang Lili: The water would be boring without these stones; it becomes alive with them. I feel somewhat enlivened by this idea as it's not common to decorate a water surface with stones in this way. You can picture the stone as a fish, a cloud, or as any living thing in the water. It seems to have a little bit of an oriental garden feeling, very poetic indeed. I think China is a country with a poet temperament.

Zhu Pei: Yes, the earliest gardens in China followed the layout of "a pool with three artificial hills," so the artistic conception was very poetic. Because water reflects the sky, buildings, and the surrounding natural environment, all of which are integrated on the water surface, the bamboo forests, water, and wood—especially when it is drizzling—all become very poetic.

Fang Lili: This is a type of emotional appeal that cannot be experienced through a visual sense alone. Therefore, it is necessary to mobilize all the senses, including sight, sound, touch, and even taste, and then experience and feel with the whole heart and soul. This is the crux of oriental aesthetics.

Zhu Pei: I think the five senses of humans shape our understanding of architecture, and we can only be touched when we use all the five senses. Architecture needs to have a chemistry with the human body, so this museum is not only for porcelain, but also for reinventing the consanguinity of the kilns, the people, and porcelain. There are porcelain museums where you can go in and view porcelains on exhibition, but there are no other factors that make you want to "talk" with the building, so as to understand the broader historical scene beyond just the porcelain itself. What is interesting and successful about this building is that it stimulates your thinking. It has empty spaces that encourage you to imagine and contemplate; it has a lot of gray space for imagination. You will see light and hear the sound of the wind from time to time. You can see that the sunken courtyard has bamboo forests, as well as contains ancient ruins discovered after construction. All these things, interwoven together, enrich people's thoughts.

Fang Lili: Here, we can see the light, the water, and the ruins; we can hear the sound of water flowing, and even footsteps that seem to echo from ancient times. The sounds and the atmosphere lend a sense of history, and a sense of place that is closely linked with nature.

Time and Space Architecture, Imagery Architecture

Fang Lili: I think this building is a very typical contemporary architecture, perhaps even an architecture with a global perspective. Modernism is the outcome of the expansion of industrialization and its goal is to create an international style; currently, human beings are entering a time of cultural scenes and space compression with a global perspective. If we say that the modernism period reflects a cubic box-like international style based on the expansion of industrialization, a cultural scenario with compressed time and space under a global outlook tends to reflect a re-localized contemporary style. This so-called re-localization seems to highlight local and native traits, though not in a traditional sense, but more along a global outlook. To put it plainly, today's Jingdezhen is no longer Jingdezhen itself, or even the Jingdezhen of China, but a Jingdezhen of the world. This is the concept of re-localization—it lengthens time and expands space, and also condenses time and space to a point. In my opinion, the design of the Imperial Kiln Museum is just like this. In terms of time, it is a museum that concentrates the history of more than 600 years around the Imperial Kilns of Ming and Qing dynasties. In terms of space, the porcelains of Jingdezhen made during ancient China's Ming and Qing dynasties are exhibited in major museums all over the world. (Of course, this is still the place of origin.) During the Ming and Qing dynasties, especially the Age of Exploration, Jingdezhen was not only making porcelain for the royal nobles of China, but also for the aristocrats of many countries in the world. The Imperial Kilns made porcelain for Chinese emperors, and the civilian kilns made porcelain for the royal nobles of other countries. In the Ming and Qing dynasties, there was much trade and interaction between officials and civilians, and the technology from the Imperial Kilns was transferred to the civilian kilns through the movement of potters, which enhanced the reputation of Jingdezhen within the world as a porcelain factory for Chinese emperors. During the Qing dynasty, officials worked with civilians to make porcelain, so many imperial porcelains were also fired in civilian kilns. How do you interpret the museum to reflect a history of hundreds of years and such a global cultural span?

Zhu Pei: Although there were many royal or royal-related porcelain wares during the Ming and Qing dynasties, I did not want to display too many here. I want the museum to present only a small amount of porcelain; less is more. The building is not intended to show porcelain, but to show its correlation with the world around it; I call it a borderless museum. Many museums in the world display Jingdezhen porcelain, and their collections of Jingdezhen porcelain may far exceed that in Jingdezhen, such as the British Museum (United Kingdom), Victoria and Albert Museum (London, United Kingdom), Metropolitan Museum of Art (United States), and Staatliche Kunstsammlungen Dresden (Dresden State Art Museum; Dresden, Germany). Porcelain from Jingdezhen Imperial Kilns or porcelain related to Imperial Kilns are scattered all over the world today, but they all come from here. The purpose of building such a museum is not to show off our collection of porcelain, but to tell a story about where porcelain comes from; to trace the origin of a civilization, and to convey to the people that the museum we see today sits right on the edge of the Imperial Kilns of the past, so that people can come here to visit historical sites and allow their imagination to wander. Therefore, this museum is not like a traditional museum, which contains a lot of collections, nor is it a pure carrier of information. It is more about offering people that path for imagination. If we seek information, we do not need to go to the museum, we can do it by surfing the internet with our mobile phones. The uniqueness of this museum is that it is located in Jingdezhen, right next to the Imperial Kiln ruins.

You see the sunken courtyard filled with sunlight; and through the bamboo forests you see museum staff repairing porcelain shards; this is another important part of the exhibition, and it's interesting for people to see the restoration process.

Fang Lili: A wonderful idea. In addition, I think the most characteristic aspect of your building is the combination of the ground level with the underground, and the space underneath the ground being larger than the space above. The space is, therefore, vast and more integrated. Why is that?

Zhu Pei: I designed it this way because I wanted to make the space on the ground a little bit lower. Once the space on the ground is high, it is no longer like a traditional brick kiln. In fact, the traditional brick kiln is also divided into two parts—an upper part and a lower part, where the two are divided by a wooden platform, with the lower part used for displaying. This meant that only a smaller scale would be suitable to represent the traditional brick kiln seen from the perspective of the ground. Traditional residential houses are 26 feet (8 meters) high, I hope that the museum can create a feeling of neighborliness with other houses. That is why people feel that the silhouette of the buildings is like the curve of hills, as if the building is lying horizontally as half of it is hidden underground.

Traditional museums are, generally, designed into a giant volume, isolated from the surroundings. But this museum is in harmony with the surrounding environment—the vaults are like little boats and very loosely placed here. They are well integrated with the surrounding environment and they interact with each other in a complementary way, which seems to keep all elements in harmony.

The museum has a main circulation route featuring permanent exhibitions, and another route for temporary exhibitions, each with its own independent entrance and exit, and which can either join or deviate from the main circulation route. Just now, we visited the café, teahouse, gift shop, bookstore, and the other service spaces. They are all organically joined to the exhibition space, weaving and blending with each other. You will see that the architecture is not frozen music, but flowing music.

The stairs here are unusual, different from what we have seen before, creating a unique experience for us. They are all embedded in between the two vaults. Natural light cascades noticeably onto the double-curved vaults built with new bricks and old kiln bricks with "kiln sweat" (a crystallized glaze). They tempt you to stop, to watch, and to touch, tracing the old bricks with your fingers and wondering about their origin and the ages when they were made, spinning daydreams and nostalgic fantasies.

Fang Lili: "Kiln sweat" is a very good term. In Jingdezhen, the internal chamber of a traditional kiln had to be rebuilt every two or three years. During the process, old bricks had to be removed. These old bricks can no longer be used to build kilns. But Jingdezhen people are good at recycling. They built houses with these bricks, therefore, the traditional local-style dwellings in the *lilongs* were all old-kiln-brick houses. "Kiln sweat" is a glaze on the brick that would come about only when it has been burnt many times in the kiln at very high temperatures. In a way, it can also be described as a crystallization of history. At present, new houses are being built everywhere in Jingdezhen, and these old kiln bricks removed from old houses can be seen everywhere. You have used them very wisely, mixing the new bricks with the old bricks; people wouldn't know which house or when (in time) a certain kiln brick comes from. People can't help but reach out to touch them, and in the process, they feel like they are entering a long tunnel of history.

Zhu Pei: The tradition of reusing old kiln bricks has continued since ancient times to today. Old as it is, it is a very new and ecological concept. The reflections you see on the glass and water keep the building in dialogue with nature, and the light is constantly changing.

Fang Lili: I saw many round glass holes at the top. It is very beautiful and gives people a very special feeling. I think you are displaying the fire holes on a traditional kiln, which is very novel and interesting. Walking inside the building is like a walk inside a traditional brick kiln, or being in the *lilongs* of Jingdezhen. There are cracks in the interval, with light cascading in and natural wind coming through. It's beautiful and mysterious. When we walk inside, it feels like we are going through a time tunnel, from ancient times to the present, with a sense of history and fresh inspiration. I think it's very interesting that you have interwoven the ground and the underground. Such a layout is not frequently seen.

Zhu Pei: Every platform that connects the ground and the underground, in fact, represents a feeling. When you look back at the building, the light from the sky illuminating this small staircase is very soft and mild. This feeling is closely related to the porcelain, and also to the kiln. In general,

I think this building gives a feeling of simplicity and originality, not of extravagant decoration. The stairs are also simple-looking. When we walk along the main circulation route, we naturally return to the original place, which is the foyer. Another surprise awaits, which is the amazing academic auditorium, which looks like a church and a spiritual space.

Fang Lili: There are also ruins scattered around, and there are steps going up. We can sit on the steps and look at the ruins.

Zhu Pei: My idea is, when you come here, the ruins tempt you to sit and linger, to take in the desolation and melancholy of the scenery, which is nothing short of compelling and beautiful. This is when you can understand the building. The ruins tell the story of the underground; through the horizontal slit in the wall, you can observe the ground as well. The ruins in front of us were discovered during construction. In order to preserve the site, we completely revised our design and finally embedded it into the museum building. The difference in height creates an outdoor theater that can shield the sun and rain. We can sit down here and experience the true essence of the museum. We can see the exterior and the interior from here; it's a semi-outdoor space. That place is both a staircase and a theater. I don't want to define its specific function. Visitors can, of course, regard it as a staircase. It can also, perhaps, be a space where students can sit and listen to their teacher tell the story of the Imperial Kilns.

Fang Lili: It is interesting to see the world outside from inside here. It's a very different experience.

Zhu Pei: When you visit the museum with your students, you can sit here, even sip tea. You can feel the wind blowing through the round-shaped kiln and later enjoy the exhibitions underneath. The museum connects the residential houses in the distance and the ruins right before us—although the surroundings are a little messy, they are real.

Fang Lili: The traditional function of a museum is to allow visitors in to view the exhibits. As for the architecture, people don't pay much attention to it because most museums are basically similar, with the same layout and the same type of lights and furnishings. People can barely capture a sense of special regional culture. But your design breaks this tradition. We can almost feel the stories that are narrated by the museum, of the local history and culture, even without the exhibits. The space inside and outside the museum itself is the carrier of the local history and culture and people come in not only to capture the visual information, but to also feel and experience things in a broader context. It can be said that the Imperial Kiln Museum was designed to arouse imagination, creativity, and help viewers frame their unique and various perceptions of Jingdezhens' Imperial Kilns through sight, sound, and touch. This is a very advanced design concept. Currently, the museum is featuring exhibitions that are mostly architecture and contemporary art. I am told the real exhibits have not come in yet. What will be on display here in the future?

Zhu Pei: Future exhibitions here will consist of two parts: One will be a permanent exhibition, comprising fragments excavated from the kiln ruins, which have been restored and joined to present the original shapes and patterns of the porcelain; and the other will be exchange or temporary exhibitions, which are still to be arranged. All this space, which is empty now, will be utilized in the future. However, I would like to keep the exhibits to a small size, leaving some empty space.

Fang Lili: Emptiness can be interesting. Not packing it too full to leave some degree of emptiness for visitors to kindle their imagination and plait their own experience would be engaging. Conventional museums mainly exist as "containers" for exhibits, which means the buildings only serve to display the contents inside. It is the "capacity," not the form of the container that really matters. So, when people go inside, they generally do not pay attention to the building itself. But your design of the museum is an exhibit itself. Every brick; every space; each beam of light from the top; the surrounding bamboo forests; the gravel paths that crunch under people's steps; the babbling brook; feet seen at ground level, that seem to wade through the water—all remind people of the Imperial Kilns and the life of Jingdezhen's craftspeople from long before. With such associations, when we look at the restored exhibits from the Imperial Kilns of the Ming and Qing dynasties, we will have a deeper understanding, as well as work up a thirst for deeper knowledge and further exploration. Here, the building is not only a container, but also a part of the exhibition, and even displays a sense of vitality and soul to the greatest extent.

Zhu Pei: Yes, the museum fully encompasses many behaviors yet to be defined and discovered, which rely on viewers' imagination, or on future generations who can give full play to their imaginations. Together, they can advance the museum into different eras. The museum must be alive, but its life is not given by its architect, but by the empty space in the museum that is left to others and to the world to interpret. For example, Chinese paintings, especially landscape paintings of the Yuan dynasty, had several concepts and "rules." First, when painting mountains, the painter never sat in front of the mountains to paint. He traveled for several months, returned home, and then painted his experience and perception. The painting is not a concrete representation of a thing, but an expression of inner feelings and experiences. What he painted was never Mount Huangshan, nor Mount Huashan, but the mountain in his heart. In such landscape paintings, nature is the most important. In the corner of the picture, he would draw a small hut to imply that the world painted on the canvas was a civilized world, not a primitive world. He knew the priority in the relationship between human civilization and nature. Second, the painting had to be completed freehand and abstractly; it was not the reappearance of a physical phenomenon, nor the reoccurrence of some scenario at that moment, but a comprehensive reflection of the journey of those last months. Third, the painting would almost always be incomplete. There was always empty space within it. One could say that the emptiness represents a fog, but what is behind the fog? It was up to people to imagine, not just the people in his time, but also the many generations that would come after, to this day, even. These works have traversed Yuan dynasty and present day and have been communicating with people through different times. Take, for instance, a European painting during the Renaissance. It emphasized a particular moment and contributed only to that moment, as a real record of a physical phenomenon, and so it ended there regardless of its perfect techniques. It was complete and, therefore, unable to communicate. As much as we admire and appreciate it, we cannot "enter" it, because all the elements have been defined, leaving no empty space for us to "wander around" in. It's the same with architecture. A very complete architecture, like some of the European Renaissance paintings, is hard for people to "enter." Of course, it is still a physical space to accommodate people's bodies, but their thoughts and imagination are restrained and left outside. This is the architecture I am not in favor of.

The concept of "Architecture of Nature" that I put forward means to make architecture incomplete, just like the Chinese paintings; to leave empty space. If it's too "complete," we can't communicate with it. The empty space in the building should be filled with flexible contents; with people's imagination, rather than predetermined elements. For example, this space—it can either be presented as a staircase, from which you can ascend from the first floor to the second floor, or it can even be viewed as a theater, where people can sit and discuss the ruins before them, or it can simply serve as a compelling spot at which to take a rest and daydream. Throughout the building, there are many places like this, either in the form of stairs or something else, where people's behaviors can deviate, and they will inevitably use these areas creatively, based on their own needs.

Fang Lili: Wonderful. In fact, you are talking about two value systems and the corresponding aesthetic choices. At first, I wondered why you put forward the concept of "Architecture of Nature." I thought it was a concept of ecology, of how a building correlated with nature and with the local historical and cultural context. But after hearing your elaboration, I understand that it, in fact, reflects the different philosophies between Eastern and Western civilizations. I think it is very clever that you compare Chinese landscape paintings with European Renaissance paintings to illustrate the different aesthetic pursuits and values of the East and the West.

Chinese landscape paintings are basically the highest level of oriental painting form. The painters show natural scenery superficially, but also on a deep level; they are expressing artistic conception, fun, and the imagery. The Chinese character "*yi*" has profound implications, which involve an extension and expansion of life and a constant overflow of soul. Therefore, it needs empty space. Chinese freehand paintings usually leave empty space, which can be more important and splendid than the brushwork elsewhere. The splendor lies in the empty space, which is left to the viewers to feel, interpret, and communicate with, allowing generations of people to use their imaginations based on the era they live in. This is referred to as the theory of "exchange" in art anthropology.

This results in a value of the artwork that is not static. It is reinterpreted and revalued through the exchange and communication between people of different eras and regions. Therefore, the artwork becomes a living "being." Your work is just like this. It provides us with infinite space for interpretation, imagination, and constant re-creation.

In addition, you mentioned that Western classical paintings were too "complete" to leave room for imagination. After modernism, the West began to witness the development of Expressionism, Fauvism, Cubism, Abstract Expressionism, and so on, and later, there were Dadaism and Installation Art. I think they were seeking to break away from being too perfect and complete. However, they took a different path, that is, the rebellion and criticism against tradition. Their expression was often intense and exaggerated, expressing tension and shock, which is different from the poetic, tranquil, and empty incompleteness and imperfection that was displayed in the East. Therefore, I often feel that whether we create, paint, or build, we are ultimately expressing philosophy. Of course, in philosophy, the East and the West are not always opposite to each other, there are definitely overlaps.

Zhu Pei: Yes, Chinese landscape paintings have a great influence on my concept of architecture, and so do Western paintings. Leonardo da Vinci's early sketches, for example, are fascinating because they are incomplete and thus open to imagination. Another example is his representative work, *Mona Lisa*, which is still very popular till today. The work itself creates mystery and suspense, leaving ample space for imagination. I think you are right when you say that oriental culture has a sense of mystery. This is because our philosophy is based on natural philosophy, which conveys a deep reverence for nature.

Fang Lili: This is the Chinese concept, so the Chinese created landscape paintings in which nature is the main body and human beings play a very small supporting role. In Western paintings, people are always the leading role. Although there are also landscape paintings in the West, they often represent a certain scene or a spot in the civilized world, and nature is only the supporting role for humankind.

Conclusion

That was a conversation between Professor Zhu Pei, an architect, and myself, an art anthropologist. Although it was a conversation between people from cross-over disciplines, there were no barriers or misunderstandings. I have realized that whatever the subject may be, within the scope of philosophy and aesthetics, we are living in a free realm, in which people can break boundaries and exchange their ideas freely without restrictions. As highlighted, human society is undergoing great changes, and human beings' aesthetic consciousness and the way that people view the world are also different today from what they used to be. Because of this, the function and mission of museums are changing as well. In such a context, the Imperial Kiln Museum designed by Professor Zhu Pei not only revolutionizes the aesthetic form, but also delves deeper into the utilization of functions and philosophical thinking.

His philosophy of "Architecture of Nature" not only brings us visual, auditory, tactile, and psychological feelings, but also leaves space to fill, to perfect, to imagine, communicate, and recreate. Adding to that, the museum is a space that includes features of regional history, culture, and natural environment; all together, these elements represent the spirituality and soul of the local context, and exist as preconditions for the city's legitimacy.

In other words, the Imperial Kiln Museum will remain an important part of the reconstruction of the city's cultural landscape for long, as well as a symbol of the arrival of another era in Jingdezhen. During the Ming and Qing dynasties, the establishment of the royal kiln factories changed the destiny of Jingdezhen and turned it into the center of urban development, but industrialization ended its specific functional value. For quite some time, people tried to discard and disguise the Imperial Kiln Factory as a backward feudal culture, demolishing the original buildings to build in its place complexes representing the new local government.

However, in recent times, as people rediscovered the Imperial Kiln's historical significance, they invited Professor Zhu Pei to design a new museum with clear contemporary expressions. It marks the arrival of a new era, which is closely linked with Jingdezhen people's future destiny. With the Imperial Kiln Museum, Professor Zhu Pei has written a footnote for this era by designing such an epoch-making building that will be an important part of Jingdezhen in the future; and he himself is destined to be a very important figure in Jingdezhen's history.

Fang Lili

Fang Lili is president of the China Society for Anthropology of Arts, deputy director of the Institute of Art Anthropology, Chinese National Academy of Arts, distinguished chief professor of the School of Art, Southeast University, director of the Institute of Art Anthropology and Sociology, Southeast University, member of the Chinese Intangible Cultural Heritage Committee, and consultant to the National Commission for the People's Republic of China for UNESCO.

Biography of Zhu Pei

Zhu Pei was born in Beijing and studied at Tsinghua University and University of California, Berkeley, and later founded Studio Zhu Pei in Beijing in 2005. From there, he has produced an extraordinary corpus of cultural works that have made him one of the leading figures of his generation. Marked by his American experience, which includes teaching as a visiting professor at Harvard and Columbia Universities, he is the current dean and professor of the School of Architecture at the Central Academy of Fine Arts (CAFA), and a visiting professor at Yale University. He was recognized as an Honorary Fellow of the American Institute of Architects (AIA) for his contribution to architecture and he was a jury member for the Mies van der Rohe Awards.

Zhu Pei's experimental works and research are dedicated to contemporary architecture, art, and the field of culture. He consistently explores the importance and relations between the root that grounds the work deeply into a specific nature and culture, and the innovation that defines the revolutionary thinking of architecture as art. Along with his experimental practice and teaching, he developed his own architectural philosophy: "Architecture of Nature." It not only encompass the poetics of construction culture, but also respond to the challenges of global climate change and regional culture rupture.

Zhu Pei's works have been exhibited at world-renowned museums like the Museum of Modern Art (MoMA) (Manhattan, United States), GA Gallery (Tokyo, Japan), Centre Pompidou (Paris, France), Victoria and Albert Museum (London, United Kingdom), Staatliche Kunstsammlungen Dresden (Dresden State Art Museum; Dresden, Germany), and MAXXI Museum (Rome, Italy); and featured in exhibitions like Venice Biennial, Sao Paulo Art Biennial, the solo exhibition at Aedes Architecture Forum, Chinese Public Art in Kassel, and even at Harvard University. His works have also been collected by MoMA, Centre Pompidou, Victoria and Albert Museum, M+ (Kowloon, Hong Kong, China), and Carnegie Museum of Art (Pittsburgh, United States).

Zhu Pei has also been commemorated and recognized with some of architecture's most prestigious awards and honors, which include: Design Vanguard Award from *Architectural Record*, AR Future Project Award from *The Architectural Review*, the Honor Award in the AIA International 2021 Design Awards, "Culture" category winner in The PLAN Award 2021, grand prize winner in Brick Award 22, "Museum" category winner in 2021 Architizer's A+Awards, 1949–2009 Grand Design Award of The Architectural Society of China, and Special Merit Award from UIA and UNESCO.

He has also been invited by many internationally renowned architecture schools to give lectures: Harvard Graduate School of Design; Columbia University's Graduate School of Architecture, Planning and Preservation (GSAPP); University of California, Berkeley; University of Cambridge; University of California, Los Angeles; Rhode Island School of Design; Syracuse University; The Cooper Union for the Advancement of Science and Art; University of South California; Southern California Institute of Architecture; University of Texas at Austin; University of New York at Buffalo; University of Illinois at Urbana-Champaign; School of Architecture at Taliesin in Taliesin West, Arizona; University of Auckland; and Tsinghua University, among others.

Project Information

Project name	Jingdezhen Imperial Kiln Museum
Location	187 Zhushan Middle Road, Zhushan District, Jingdezhen City, Jiangxi Province, China
Client	Jingdezhen Municipal Bureau of Culture Radio Television Press Publication and Tourism, Jingdezhen Ceramic Culture Tourism Group
Design period	January 2016–March 2017
Construction period	October 2016–March 2020
Site area	104,970 square feet (9,752 square meters)
Total floor area	111,621 square feet (10,370 square meters)
Structure	Reinforced-concrete arch shell and brick arch
Architecture, interior, and landscape design	Studio Zhu Pei
In-charge (design)	Zhu Pei
Critic	Zhou Rong
Art consultants	Wang Mingxian, Li Xiangning
Design team	He Fan, Shuhei Nakamura, Han Mo, You Changchen, Zhang Shun, Liu Yian, Liu Ling, Wu Zhigang, Du Yang, Yang Shengchen, Chen Yida, He Chenglong, Ding Xinyue, Nie Wenhao
Cooperative design in architecture and landscape	Architectural Design and Research Institute of Tsinghua University
Cooperative design in interior and exhibition	Studio Zhu Pei, Beijing Qingshang Architectural Ornamental Engineering Co., Ltd, Academy of Arts and Design, Tsinghua University

General contractor	China Construction First Group Corporation Limited, Huajiang Construction Co., Ltd of China Construction First Group
Structural, MEP, and green building	Architectural Design and Research Institute, Tsinghua University
Façades	Shenzhen Dadi Facade Technology Co., Ltd
Lighting	Ning Field Lighting Design Co., Ltd
Acoustics	Building Science and Technology Institute, Zhejiang University
Showcase	Sichuan Province Click Netherfield Exhibition and Display Co., Ltd
Photography	Su Shengliang: front cover, 121, 122, 123, 124-125, 126–127, 128-129, 138, 139, 140, 141, 142-143, 144, 145, 146-147, 148, 150, 151, 152, 153, 155, 156, 157, 158, 159, 160 (left), 161, 162-163, 164, 166, 167, 168-169, 170, 171, 175, 178, 179; Tian Fangfang: 114–115, 136-137, 149; Jin Weiqi: 135 (bottom), 190, 191, 192, 193, 195, 196, 197, 198-199, 200, 201, 202, 203, 204; Zhang Qinquan: 172–173; Chen Yaojie: 205; Zhang Xi: 8 (left); Dong Botai: 8 (right); Studio Zhu Pei: 45, 46, 47, 48, 49, 50, 51, 53, 54, 55, 64, 65, 66-67, 68, 69, 70, 71, 72, 73, 74, 75, 76, 77, 78, 79, 80, 81, 96, 97, 98, 99, 100, 101, 102-103, 120, 130-131, 132-133, 134, 135 (top), 154, 160 (right), 165, 174, 176, 177, 194, 238, back cover
Recognition and awards	Honor Award, AIA International 2021 Design Awards "Culture" category winner, The PLAN Award 2021 Project of the Year and "Museum" category winner, 2021 Architizer A+Awards "Architecture—Buildings Over 1,000 SqM" category winner, 2021 AZ Awards Grand prize winner and "Sharing Public Spaces" category winner, Brick Award 22 First prize, Architectural Design Award (2019–2020) of the Architectural Society of China "Cultural Regeneration" category winner, The Architectural Review Future Project Awards 2017 "Top 10 Museums and Cultural Venues" selected by *designboom* in 2020 "Top 10 Museums and Galleries" selected by *Dezeen* in 2020

Acknowledgments

The idea of this book was inspired by encouragement from many scholars to reveal the ideology behind the creation process of the Jingdezhen Imperial Kiln Museum. First and foremost, I would like to extend my deepest appreciation to Professor Wang Mingxian for his help and valuable advice in the conception of this book.

I would like to acknowledge remarkable scholars Kenneth Frampton, Steven Holl, Arata Isozaki, Rem Koolhaas, Mohsen Mostafavi, and Thomas Krens, as well as great Chinese scholars Fan Di'an, Wang Mingxian, Zhou Rong, Li Xiangning, and Fang Lili for contributing their inspiring critique on this book; their words inspired me in various ways, the book would not be what it is without their enthusiastic help.

I would like to express my particular gratitude to Professor Kenneth Frampton who generously discussed the ideas on the Imperial Kiln Museum with me to offer his critique and opinions on the conceptual design when I was teaching at Columbia University in 2016. I also wish to acknowledge the on-site observation and suggestions made by Zhou Rong, Fang Lijun, Mohsen Mostafavi, Li Xiangning, and Aric Chen.

I am deeply indebted to artists Xu Bing, Sui Jianguo, and Liu Xiaodong who participated in the opening exhibition of the Imperial Kiln Museum. Their outstanding artworks have enabled the Imperial Kiln Museum to expand its own boundaries.

I am also grateful to my colleagues Chang Zhigang, Zheng Yawen, He Keren, and Huang Liangfu from CAFA (Central Academy of Fine Arts) who have been supportive in the planning and proofreading of the English print of this book. I am enormously grateful for their generous help.

I am similarly deeply appreciative of the dedication of my colleagues Xia Yaoyao and Liu Yian who have been especially helpful in their outstanding contributions toward the creativity, data sorting, editing, typesetting design, and text translation of this book. I am grateful for their patience and perseverance in the face of such complicated and tedious work.

I would also like to thank Chen Dijia for the effort provided to translate the articles "Preface: Zhu Pei's Architecture," "Zhu Pei's Jingdezhen Imperial Kiln Museum in Jiangxi, China 2016–2020," and "The Archaeology of a Museum" from English to Chinese. I also wish to thank my students Wang Wen, Zhang Xi, Wang Siqi, Wang Junqi, and Wang Yiru for their extraordinary work in reviewing the literature and text translation of this book, and Xuan Qidong who has contributed greatly in guiding the visual design of this book. I would like to express my sincere thanks to photographers Su Shengliang, Tian Fangfang, Jin Weiqi, and Zhang Qinquan who have contributed excellent photographs of the Jingdezhen Imperial Kiln Museum and wish to acknowledge their generous support.

Last, but certainly not least, I am enormously grateful for the generous help from the publishers, editors, and printers: Guangxi Normal University Press, The Images Publishing Group, and Artron Art Group, for their great support and help in the editing, publishing, and printing of this book; I take this opportunity to commend and thank every participant for their level of professional ethics, as well as unremitting efforts in this complicated work.